D1392494

SPECTACULAR SCIENCE

8 FOR YEAR OLDS

ILLUSTRATED BY AL MURPHY

GLENN MURPHY

BY THE AUTHOR OF WHY IS SNOT GREEN?

MACMILLAN CHILDREN'S BOOKS

Published 2021 by Macmillan Children's Books
an imprint of Pan Macmillan
The Smithson, 6 Briset Street, London EC1M 5NR
EU representative: Macmillan Publishers Ireland Ltd, 1st Floor,
The Liffey Trust Centre, 117–126 Sheriff Street Upper,
Dublin 1, D01 YC43
Associated companies throughout the world
www.panmacmillan.com

ISBN 978-1-5290-6529-9

1 3 5 7 9 8 6 4 2

A CIP catalogue record for this book is available from the British Library.

Printed and bound by CPI Group (UK) Ltd, Croydon CR0 4YY

MIX
Paper from
responsible sources
FSC® C116313

QUESTIONS AND ANSWERS

FROM SEAN MURPHY (AGED 7)

BY GLENN MURPHY (AGED 47)

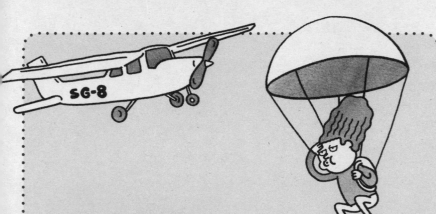

CONTENTS

ANIMALS, EVOLUTION, AND EXTINCTION

WHY DO ANIMALS HIBERNATE?

Animals hibernate to slow down their body systems and save energy. This helps them survive freezing temperatures and scarce food supplies during the cold, harsh winters. Not all animals do it, as there is a risk they will never wake up. But one day, humans may even learn to hibernate, too . . .

Whoa – hang on. Why might they never wake up? I thought hibernation was just when big animals (like bears) slept through the winter.

Sleep and hibernation are two very different things. Most animals **sleep** – resting for some part of each day or night – in order to let their bodies heal and grow, or to help their brains process memory and learning. Some –

like birds and frogs – sleep for just a few hours each day. Others – like lions and koalas – spend most of their day asleep.

There are different phases (or stages) in sleep, ranging from **daydreaming** and **light sleep**, to **deep**, **dreamless sleep**, and you generally cycle through all of these – more than once – within one night of sleeping. In all phases of sleep, your **breathing** and **blood pressure** drop a little, and the **brain** is **less active** than when you are awake. Depending on which phase of sleep you are in, your **muscles** might be **twitchy** and **active**, or **floppy** and **relaxed**. But none of these sleep states – not even deep sleep – come anywhere close to the state of **hibernation**.

So if it's not sleep, then what is it?

Hibernation is a **massive, extended shift** to an animal's body and brain state. A hibernating mammal might breathe just **once or twice per minute**, and its **heart rate** can drop to **5 beats a minute** or less. Body temperature can drop by several degrees*. Brain activity slows down, and there are few flickers or signs of dreaming. While **sleep** only lasts for a few minutes or hours, **hibernation** can last for weeks, months, or years. And while most animals can wake from sleep quickly and without harm, it can take **hours** for an animal to recover from hibernation. And if they come out of it too suddenly, they can become ill and die.

Sleep is a routine state for most animals. But hibernation is a drastic, risky business that leaves the animal limp, weak, and vulnerable to attack.

So why do they do it?

Mostly to save energy. While some animals **migrate** to escape freezing temperatures and dwindling food supplies during winter, others **stay put** and **hibernate** instead.

Dropping their heart rate helps them use less energy, allowing them to survive on the fat stores they built up during spring, summer, and autumn. And since warm-blooded animals use most of their energy just trying to keep warm in winter, dropping their core

---

* Some animals – like the Arctic ground squirrel – can actually drop their body temperature below zero degrees Celsius!

body temperature on purpose means they use their hard-earned energy stores far more slowly – over months, rather than days.

Is it only bears that do it?

Not at all. Besides bears, lots of other mammals hibernate, too – including **squirrels**, **chipmunks**, **lemurs**, and **bats**. Reptiles – like **snakes**, **lizards**, and **turtles** – are cold-blooded animals, and cannot control their body temperature the way mammals do. So when reptiles have to ride out harsh, freezing winters, they do it by burrowing underground to stay warm. This is called **brumation**.

Not all animals hibernate to escape the cold. Some desert animals do it to save energy and stay cool during the hottest, summer months. This is called **aestivation**.

And a few clever Australian mammals, like the **spiny echidna**, may dig in and hibernate during and after a **forest fire** – waiting for the land and plants to regrow before they emerge again to feed, weeks or months later.

That's pretty smart! So do humans hibernate?

Do we hibernate? No. *Can* we hibernate? Probably.

Really?

Yep. In fact, surgeons sometimes create a kind of 'emergency' hibernation state when someone suffers a severe brain injury or heart attack. If the heart stops working, or blood stops getting to the brain, then the brain typically shuts down after a few **minutes**. But at low enough temperatures, the brain can survive with little or no blood flow for **up to two hours**. So in extreme cases, the surgeon – with the help of an anaesthetist[*] – may decide to put a patient to sleep and chill their body with special cooling equipment. This buys time for the surgeon to repair the damage, and improve their chances of surviving and recovering.

Woah. But what about healthy people? Could we just hibernate through the yucky winter and enjoy the sunshine when we wake up?

....

[*] A doctor who specializes in medicines that numb the body to pain, or make you sleep while a surgeon operates.

Well, even if you could would you really want to? After all, you would be losing all those months of your life (not to mention snow days and snowball fights) – time you would never get back again.

Oh, I hadn't thought about that. I do like snowball fights.

Me, too. But there is one group of people who might be very interested in sleeping through bits of their lives – **astronauts**. NASA has been researching human hibernation (also known as **hypometabolic stasis**) for use in long-distance space travel.

As yet, the farthest we humans have travelled from Earth is about **390,000 km (240,000 miles)** – the average distance to the **moon**. With current spacecraft technologies, this takes about **six days** (three to get there, three to get back).

One day, we hope to land astronauts – maybe even settlers – on **Mars**. But Mars is over **243 million km (151 million miles) away**. The journey takes around **seven months** one way. Seven months is a long time to spend cooped up in a spaceship.

But if we ever hope to travel beyond our own solar system, to Earth-like planets in other systems elsewhere in the galaxy, then the distances and travel times get

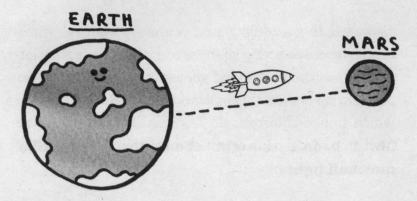

much longer. Our closest neighbouring star, Proxima Centauri, is about **4.2 light-years (40 *trillion* km)** away. It does have planets of its own. Planets that may be home to alien life. But it would take us over **73,000 years** to get there!

Oh. Yeah, that's not going to work.

Right. Now one day we may figure out how to travel much faster. Maybe even at something close to the speed of light. But even at light speed, it would still take at least **4 years** to travel to our nearest star system, or **8 years** there and back. To most people, 4 years cooped up with the same, few people would feel like being in **prison**.

But what if you could sleep through the 7-month journey to Mars, or take a 4-year nap and wake up in another star system? And what if by slowing down your metabolism, you hardly **aged** during that time, either?

These are the questions that NASA and human stasis researchers are trying to answer. Using a combination of sleep drugs, feeding tubes, and special 'hibernation pods', they have already proved it can work in **rats** – which unlike squirrels, do not usually hibernate. The next step would be to test it on humans. If, that is, they can find any volunteers . . .

Hmmmm. Not sure I'd want to be the one to test it. But if they got it working . . .

You'd be straight on the next flight to Mars?

Totally! Wait – do they have Xboxes on Mars?

SUPER-SNOOZERS

Bears are famous for hibernating through the winter. But they are by no means alone in the super-sleeping game. Here are 8 more animals that hibernate – and how long they do it.

Bats – 6 months: Not all bats hibernate – some (like fruit bats) live in warm places, and others migrate to warmer climes during winter instead. Those species that do hibernate hide up in caves, attics, or tree-holes from October through March.

Bumblebees – 6–7 months: Ever wonder where they go in the winter? Every bee in a colony (except the queen) dies as winter sets in. But the queen hibernates, survives, and emerges to start a new colony in the spring.

Chipmunks – 4 months: As winter sets in, chipmunks dig a small, 3-foot-deep burrow and snooze lightly through the colder months, waking up intermittently to graze on stored snacks.

Geckos – 3–4 months: These small, sticky-footed reptiles hole up inside caves, crevices, or rotting logs, storing fat in their tails ahead of the long winter sleep.

Hedgehogs – 6 weeks–6 months: Hedgehogs dig burrows, or hide and snooze in wood piles, compost heaps, or old sheds through the colder months. Depending on where they live, they might only hibernate for 6 weeks, or as long as 6 months.

Hummingbirds – 1 week–3 months: Though they typically avoid colder climates altogether, hummingbirds have such tiny bodies (and such high energy use) that they hang upside down and stop moving around through the cooler weeks and months in some habitats.

Ladybirds – 3–4 months: Ladybirds hibernate lightly and in groups – preferring warm, comfortable spots like the cracks around windows and doorways.

Snails – up to 3 years: Many land snails hibernate to prevent their slimy, watery bodies from freezing in harsh winters. When a local cold snap persists, some snails can stay inside their shells for up to 3 years without food or water.

ACTIVITY: SUPER-SLEEPERS

List a number of species from each major animal family, i.e. whales, bears and squirrels (mammals), butterflies, ladybirds and ants (insects), geese, chickens and penguins (birds), and snakes, turtles and chameleons (reptiles).

Now think about the patterns of behaviour each animal has over the course of a year.

- What do they do each winter?

- Which animals hibernate?

- Which animals migrate?

- Which animals adapt, or stay in place to gather food?

- Which ones grow winter coats or plumage?

Make a chart of which animals **hibernate**, **migrate** or **adapt**, using information from science books or science websites to help you.

HOW DO ANIMALS GO EXTINCT?

Species can go extinct in lots of different ways, including sudden or gradual changes to their habitats, new and catastrophic diseases, being hunted to extinction by predators, and being pushed out of existence by rival species. All animal species eventually go extinct. In fact, most already have.

What do you mean, *all* animals go extinct? That can't be right. Or else there would be no animals left . . .

All species do eventually go extinct. According to biologists, 99–98% of all species on Earth – including plants, animals, fungi, and microbes – has already gone extinct. But thankfully, they didn't all go at once. Rather, each species appears, survives for a time, then eventually disappears. How long they get to stick around for varies quite a bit. Most mammal species have an average lifespan of 1–2 million years on Earth, but they usually belong to a group of very similar species that survive for far longer. The modern **giraffe**, for example, is possibly just **1 million years** old, but giraffes have been around for at least **8 million** years. Meanwhile, the **duck-billed platypus**'s first duck-billed relatives appeared at least **60 million** years ago!

Whoa! Platypuses are even cooler than I thought!

Yup. And mammals are one of the newest (i.e. most recent) forms of life on the planet. Others have been around way longer. **Horseshoe crabs** have survived for over **400 million** years, and **comb jellyfish**, for over **600 million** years – making both of those groups older than the dinosaurs (almost all of which lived between 250 million and 65 million years ago). But these hardcore, long-

lived survivors are the rare, lucky ones, and even they will one day disappear, too. What we *do not* see is the thousands of other mammals, crustaceans, and jellyfish that went extinct along the way.

So what happens to all those species? Do they just self-destruct or something?

Species can go extinct in lots of different ways. In fact, you might say that there are a lot more ways to die than there are ways to live!

One obvious path to species loss is being **eaten**, or **hunted** to death. The **dodo**, the **passenger pigeon**, and the **woolly mammoth** all likely met their end this way. In addition to hunting, animals brought to Mauritius by humans also ate dodo eggs, which didn't help.

Another obvious way to go is **starvation** – not just of a few animals, but of an entire species. If plant life suddenly disappears in an area, then the **herbivores** that depend on it will die off, and the **carnivores** that prey on them will die off, too. This can happen after a **drought**, **fire**, or **natural disaster** kills off **all the plant life** in an area, or when a new disease kills off a **specific plant** that one or more herbivores depend upon. Koalas and pandas, for example, eat only eucalyptus and bamboo (respectively). If those plant species were wiped out by some new plant virus, then koalas and pandas would be wiped out, too. Thankfully, that has never happened. But it could.

What about fighting over territory? Could that kill off a species?

Animals fight over territory and resources all the time, but usually they reach some sort of balance, and find ways to share and coexist with other animals in the area. Cheetahs, lions, hyenas, and hunting dogs, for example, all hunt similar prey on the plains and grasslands of Africa. But all these species have survived for millions of years, as for the most part, they find ways to avoid and tolerate each other.

However, sometimes an alien species may arrive in an area, and be so much better at hunting or grazing that it **outcompetes** all the species that have been there for thousands of years.

Wait – you mean *actual* aliens?

Not as in 'extra-terrestrial alien', no. As in 'a **foreign species**' – one not born to that country or habitat*. These **invasive species** can wreak havoc in their new environments, munching through plant life faster than

---

* Although I guess actual aliens could one day arrive from space and outcompete us, too. For an idea of what that might look like, see H. G. Wells' classic tale *The War of the Worlds*, or any number of alien-invasion movies.

it can grow back, or wiping out whole populations of prey animals not used to being hunted by them. Examples include **rabbits** brought to Australia by European settlers, which damaged crops and wiped out entire orchards and forests by multiplying and overgrazing. **Wild pigs** (or boar) are an invasive species brought to the USA (also by Europeans) for sport-hunting – which now run wild as feral boar, uprooting crops, destroying forests, and carrying diseases like pseudorabies to native animals.

Meanwhile, pet **Burmese pythons** released into the wild have wiped out 90% of small mammals in Florida's swamps and forests. Some of these 6 m (20 foot) swamp-monsters have been eating deer, foxes, pet cats and dogs.

Yikes! Wouldn't want to meet one of those.

It is important to realize, though, that while hunting, natural disasters, competition, and invading aliens are all dramatic ways to go extinct, the most common reasons for species loss are slower, more gradual, and less visible.

Chief among these is **habitat loss** – or the loss of home territory within which an animal can live, feed, and breed. Human logging wiped out many of the natural forests of Europe, and has destroyed nearly **1.3 million square kilometres** (**500,000 square miles**) of natural forest since 1990. In all, humans have cut down close to **half** the **total number of trees** on the planet. That means tigers, jaguars, lemurs, orangutans and forest birds are being squashed into far smaller spaces – and many of these species are now endangered as a result.

Climate change and **pollution** are driving many species to extinction, too. **Climate change** is both accelerating habitat loss, and putting pressure on animals themselves – as plant and animal species find it hard to adapt to shifting temperatures. **Pollution** can poison entire rivers, lakes and oceans, and lay waste to entire species of fish, dolphin, or seabird.

That seems so sad. All those animals, gone for good.

It certainly can be, yes. Some of the most fantastic and incredible creatures that ever lived have long since been lost to past changes in climate, new competition, or the arrival of humans in a new part of the world (see below).

But looked at another way, extinction is also a natural and necessary process. It clears the way for new species, which might otherwise never have had a chance. Dinosaurs were amazing, and we would all love to see one. But dinosaurs also dominated the planet for

nearly 200 million years, and if they had not finally gone extinct, our small, furry, mammalian ancestors would never have had a chance to thrive, multiply, and become the wondrous variety of animals we see on Earth today. From **platypuses** and **giraffes**, to **hedgehogs**, **ring-tailed lemurs**, and **Siberian flying squirrels**.

And *us*, right?

Absolutely – us, too. Without extinction (specifically, of huge, toothy things that can eat people) we very likely would not exist. And now we humans – for the first time in the history of our planet – have a chance to be **caretakers** of other living species.

With our rare ability to observe, study, and plan ahead, we can choose to protect threatened habitats, save vulnerable and endangered species, and manage our own species' impact on this Earth. That way, we can enjoy the species we share the planet with for longer – however long that turns out to be.

So how long will *we* be around?

Well, we've only been here for a few hundred-thousand years, and the average for a mammals is a **million** years. So with a bit of luck (and no alien invasions), I'd say we've got a good run ahead of us yet.

Good. Cause I kind of like it here.

FANTASTIC CREATURES (NOW GONE)

The dinosaurs became extinct over 60 million years ago. But here are just a few of the animals we have lost to climate change, hunting, and human activities within the last few thousand years.

Thylacine (a.k.a. Tasmanian tiger) – extinct since 1930 (?)

This incredible beast looked like a cross between a tiger and a wolf, but was actually a marsupial – more closely related to kangaroos and opossums. Both male and female thylacines had stiff tails and pouches for carrying young. Though they walked on all fours like dogs, they would hop like kangaroos when alarmed or trying to move at speed. The thylacine was the top predator on the Australian island of Tasmania until humans arrived. They were thought to be extinct in the wild as of 1930, but some scientists think they may have survived through to the 1990s, or may even still be alive in remote parts of the island!

Woolly rhinoceros – extinct since 6,000 BC

Once found throughout Europe and Asia, the woolly rhino was 2 metres (6 feet) tall, 4 metres (12 feet) long, and weighed over 6 tonnes. Its thick, hairy coat made it well-adapted to the frozen northern tundra regions, and it had two horns – one small, one huge – adorning its formidable snout. Cave paintings from England to Germany and Russia suggest prehistoric humans hunted them for meat, bone, and horn, but it was probably a combination of human activity and a steadily warming climate that finished them off, around 8,000 years ago.

Sabre-toothed cat – extinct since 9,000 BC

Sabre-toothed cats prowled Europe, Asia, Africa and the Americas for over 40 million years – but around the end of the Pleistocene epoch, about 10,000 years ago, they finally died out. This was likely due to both climate change and competing with humans for prey. These huge cats were similar in size to lions, but built more thickly and powerfully, like bears. There were at least 50 species of sabre-toothed cat, including the famous *Smilodon* (dirk-toothed cat) and *Homotherium* (Scimitar-toothed cat). All 50 species had terrifyingly large canine teeth, which measured up to 30 cm (12 inches) long.

Megatherium (a.k.a. giant ground sloth) – extinct since 10,000 BC (?)

These massive mammals roamed the forests and lakes of North and South America throughout the last Great Ice Age. Most or all of them died out when that age ended, around 12,000 years ago – though some scientists think they survived for thousands of years longer on remote Caribbean islands. Unlike their modern sloth cousins, ground sloths did not live in trees, but did live among them. Fully grown, they would stand up to 3 m (10 feet) tall, weighed the same as an ox, and used their formidable claws to pull down tree branches and strip them of leaves.

COULD WE EVER BRING DINOSAURS BACK TO LIFE?

Possibly – but not the way they did it in *Jurassic Park*. Dinosaur fossils contain bone, soft tissues, even blood – but not the DNA you would need to clone them. But we may one day be able to create a dinosaur from a living relative – using something called reverse genetic engineering.

Oh, come on! Seeing a real live T. rex would be so coooool! There must be some way we could do it. Like, clone them or something?

Perhaps. We have already managed to clone more than 10 different animal species – including **rats**, **cats**, **cows**, **sheep**, and **horses**. And in December 2020, we successfully cloned an endangered **black-footed ferret** from the frozen DNA of an animal that died 30 years ago. It is hoped that with practice we might be able to protect and preserve other endangered species this way. Or maybe even bring extinct ones back from the dead.

A black-footed ferret

See?! We _can_ make new animals made from old DNA!

We can, yes. But cloning is far from easy, and if we are ever to do it with dinosaurs, we have some serious hurdles to jump over first.

Like what?

For starters, all the animals we have cloned so far were made by injecting DNA into a live, animal **egg**, then **implanting** that egg into a living, animal **mother**.

If you are cloning a **rat** or a **sheep**, that's no problem. There are plenty of rats and sheep around to work with. **Black-footed ferrets** are rare, so the cloned ferret we just talked about was made by implanting an egg injected with the DNA from a frozen black-footed ferret (called Willa) into a **domestic ferret** mother. The result was an identical genetic **clone** of Willa, which the scientist named **Elizabeth Ann**.

Elizabeth Ann – the cloned baby black-footed ferret

Awwww – she's cute!

Agreed. Ridiculously so. But here's the first problem – if you are trying to clone a **dinosaur**, you need **dinosaur DNA**. In the *Jurassic Park* books and movies, they find this inside prehistoric mosquitoes, trapped and preserved in fossilized tree sap (also known as amber), with dinoblood and DNA still inside them.

Does that not happen in real life, then?

Not all of it, no. We have found prehistoric insects trapped in amber. Some of these have been biting insects with traces of vertebrate blood (maybe mammal, maybe reptile blood) still inside them. But sadly, DNA is a pretty flimsy molecule, and it doesn't seem to last that well. The oldest piece of DNA we have found to date was about 1 million years old. But the dinosaurs died out – or evolved into other things – around 66 million years ago. So the chances of finding any dino DNA seem slim at best.

Even if we did find some – say, the perfectly preserved DNA from a long-dead *Tyrannosaurus rex* – to turn it into a living, breathing animal, we would still need a healthy **dinosaur egg** to inject the DNA into, plus a healthy **dinosaur mother** to lay the egg and hatch it. Not too many of those around, are there?

Couldn't you put the DNA in the egg of a different animal? Then put it into a mother crocodile or something?

That is actually not the craziest idea. Dinosaurs and crocodiles do share a common ancestor, and for a while, they actually shared the planet! But sadly, they are just too different for this to work. Black-footed and domestic ferrets are different species, but they are similar enough that their bodies can be tricked into carrying each other's eggs. Crocs and dinos are far further apart. In fact, the closest living relative of the dinosaurs are **birds**.

Technically, birds are a two-legged **therapod** (dinosaurs that evolved feathers, beaks, and birdy behaviours). By taking to the skies, and evolving into different shapes, they managed to avoid following the other dinosaurs into extinction.

Alright, then – let's put the dino DNA in a chicken, or a hawk. Plenty of those around.

We could try that, yes. Bird DNA seems a bit harder to work with than mammal DNA. Although we have succeeded in cloning sheep, horses, and cattle, we have yet to produce a single, measly chicken clone. So it might take us a while to figure that out. And if we plan to make dinosaurs from chickens, we would need some pretty healthy dino DNA to work with, and a good amount of luck getting bird eggs to accept it.

Sigh. So we're stuck. There's no way to do it?

I wouldn't say that. If you really wanted to make a *T. rex*, there is one other method you might try: **reverse engineering.** Or rather, **reverse *genetic* engineering**.

What's that?

Reverse engineering is when you take a machine or system you already have, and take it apart to figure out how it is built, then make your own version based on that new knowledge and understanding. If you wanted to build your own **vacuum cleaner**, for example, you could try to design one from scratch, or you could find an old one, take it apart, and examine the various parts – vacuum motor, power cord, suction tube, dust bag, and so on – and make your own versions of these to build a new one.

    Reverse *genetic* engineering is similar, only using DNA and living tissues and body parts. Let's say you want to make a **woolly mammoth** – another extinct species we could one day bring back from the dead. We have actually found **mammoth DNA** inside million-year-old mammoth molars*. More than likely, that DNA is too old and broken to clone new baby mammoths with. But DNA is like a blueprint, or a set of instructions for building an animal. So even if it's only a partial blueprint, and some of the instructions are missing, we can still study it to figure out how mammoths were put together.

How would you do that?

We know mammoths were like elephants, only **bigger**, **hairier**, and with different-shaped **skulls** and **tusks**. So in theory, if you could figure out which **genes** (or sets of DNA instructions) were different between elephants and mammoths, then you could take an elephant egg, pull out the DNA, and insert mammoth-like genes for hairy skin, bigger tusks, and massive bodies. Then you implant that genetically engineered egg into a normal elephant mother, and see if she gives birth to something like a baby mammoth.

Technically, the baby would not actually be a mammoth. It would be a transgenic elephant. Transgenic

---

* Try saying that five times really fast: million-year-old-mammoth-molars, million-year-old-mammoth-molars, million-year-old-mammoth-molars . . .

animals are ones that contain genes (or bits of DNA) that have been deliberately added from another, quite different species. There are transgenic plants, transgenic animals, and transgenic bacteria. In this case, we would be making a transgenic elephant with mammoth-like features.

Who cares?! If it looks like a mammoth, walks like a mammoth, acts like a mammoth, that's good enough for me! So could we do that with a _T. rex_ or _Velociraptor_ instead?

Possibly. Since birds and dinosaurs are so closely related, if you were lucky enough to find some patchy _T. rex_ DNA, you might compare it to that of a modern-day, birdy predator like a hawk or eagle. Then you figure out which genes code for clawed arms instead of wings, thick walking legs, rather than skinny perching ones, and toothy, crocodile-like jaws, rather than sharp beaks. And maybe delete the genes for feathers. If it worked, you would end up with a 1 metre (3 foot)-tall _T. rex_ with pink, pimply skin and a bird-like skull with teeth.

Scale up the growth genes a bit, and you might even get one to grow to 4 m (12 feet) tall or more – like the original _T. rex_ was.

Actually, that sounds pretty terrifying.

It might be, yes. Then there's the question of what you do with your new transgenic hawk-o-saurus. Where would it live? What would it eat? With the natural prey of the *T. rex* (i.e. other dinosaurs) no longer on the menu, you would have to feed it something else – like cows, goats, or antelopes. What if it escaped and went on the rampage, started attacking and eating humans? And even if you could keep if safely contained in some sort of dinosaur safari park, would it ever be happy, being the only one of its kind? Do we bring back a whole family of them, try to rebuild the species in the wilds of Africa or Australia? What would happen if we succeeded? I'm guessing there would be many fewer lions, giraffes, elephants and kangaroos left in the wild, for starters.

Hmmm – I hadn't thought about it like that. Maybe let's just stick with endangered ferrets for now. And maybe just a *little* mammoth . . .

BACK FROM THE DEAD: EXTINCT ANIMALS WE MIGHT CLONE ONE DAY

Even if we could, not everyone agrees that bringing back the *T. rex* is a good idea. But here are a few other extinct animals we may decide to resurrect first.

Elephant Bird

A giant (3 metre, 1.6 tonnes) flightless bird native to Madagascar, which died out during the medieval age, probably due to human settling, hunting, and pilfering eggs. Their eggs were over 33 cm (13 inches) tall and weighed 10 kg (22 pounds) – making them roughly 160 times larger than a chicken egg. A single egg could feed an entire family, and the broken shells were used as bowls long afterwards.

Quagga

A unique species of zebra, hunted to extinction by European settlers in South Africa in the late 1800s. With stripes only on its front half, the quagga looked like someone had glued a zebra and a horse together in the middle! The last known wild quagga died in 1878, and the last captive quagga (at a zoo in Amsterdam) died five years later.

Irish Elk (a.k.a. giant deer)

This immense Irish elk once ranged right across Eurasia – from the west coast of Ireland to the eastern tip of Siberia – but probably died out around 7,000 years ago. It stood 2 m (6 feet) tall at the shoulder and weighed over 700 kg (1.5 tonnes) – making it roughly the size of an Alaskan moose. Its magnificent antlers measured 3.7 m (12 feet) across from tip to tip, and may have made it harder for the giant deer to escape human hunters.

Great Auk

This foot-tall, flightless seabird looked much like a giant penguin, but was not closely related to modern penguins at all. It lived in the North Atlantic Ocean, from coastal Canada and Greenland to Ireland, the UK and Scandinavia. They were both hunted and revered by Native American tribes, but early European settlers to the Americas ate them, skinned them, and used them for fishing bait. The last two known auks were killed off the coast of Iceland in 1844.

Woolly Mammoth

The last known population of woolly mammoths lived on remote, frosty Wrangel Island – in the East Siberian Sea between Northern Russia and Alaska – around 4,000 years ago. But they once ranged the entire Northern hemisphere, from Europe to North America. Now scientists at Harvard University in the USA are attempting to reconstruct these long-dead animals, as part of the Woolly Mammoth Revival project. By adding mammoth genes (for hairy coats, thicker hides, and cold-adapted blood cells) to elephant embryos, they hope to create a kind of man-made mammoth by the end of the decade. The idea being to foster them in zoos for a while, then eventually releasing them into the wilds of Europe, Canada, and the USA.

WHY CAN'T ELEPHANTS AND RHINOS MAKE BABY RHINOPHANTS?

Animal hybrids – or cross-breeds – are actually quite common in nature, and cross-breeding is actually one way that new species are created. But this usually only happens between very closely related species. So while black and white rhinos can have 'grey' rhino babies, rhinophants are – sadly – off the menu. At least for now . . .

So you do get animals that are half-this, half-that?

Absolutely. Half-this, half-that animals are called **hybrids**. Dramatic, real-life hybrids include **ligers** (half lion, half tiger), **coywolves** (half coyote, half wolf), and **pizzly bears** (half polar bear, half grizzly bear).

Wait – WHAT? The liger is a real animal?!

Yep, it is.

Ligers are the result of a **male lion** breeding with a **female tiger**. The result is a giant, 3.4 m (11 foot) cat that weighs up to 400 kg (900 lbs) – with faint, tiger-like stripes on its sandy, lion-like coat (but no mane).

Coywolves look as you might expect, like coyotes with wolf-like ears and coats. Scientists are still arguing about how to group them and name them. In some places, they are known as **eastern coyotes**. In others, **eastern wolves**, or **red wolves**.

Pizzly bears happen when **polar bears** living north of Canada's Arctic Circle breed with **grizzly bears** ranging south of it. The result is a large bear with creamy-white fur, with brown patches around the legs, paws, and eyes. The first one was spotted in the wild in 2006. **Pizzlies** are also known as **grolar bears,** or **nanulaks** – which combines the Inuit words for polar bear (nanuk), and grizzly bear (aklak).

Over the years, biologists have discovered hundreds, maybe thousands, of previously undiscovered hybrid species living in the wild. Including hybrid **cats**, **dogs**, **birds**, **monkeys**, **frogs**, and **insects**. Leading some of us to believe that interbreeding between species – or

hybridization – is a lot more important for animal evolution than we once thought.

Most species change gradually over time, shaped by their environment and random mutations in their genes. But once in a while, it seems, a species can change all at once – by interbreeding with another species to create a new one.

That is just *too* cool! So if you can get ligers and pizzly bears, then why not catdogs, or rhinophants?

Good question. The thing is, hybrids usually only happen when the two cross-breeding species are very closely related.

The most reliable way to make an animal hybrid is to use two animals of the same species, with small differences between them – like fur colour. This is why you can reliably cross a **Poodle** (species: *Canis domesticus*) with a **Labrador** (species: *Canis domesticus*) to get a **Labradoodle**. Or a Cocker Spaniel with a Poodle to make a **Cockapoo**. Or – my personal favourite – a **Schnauzer** and a Poodle to get a **Schnoodle**. Lots of cross-bred dogs, cats, and rabbits are made this way. By crossing two animals of the same species, you are hardly even hybridizing at all. So it's easy.

But once you start using animals of different species – even different families – then things rarely go quite so well.

You can cross a **domestic cat** (*Felis domesticus*) with a **Serval Cat** (*Leptailurus serval*) to get a hybrid cat called a **Savannah cat** (which likes to fetch and follow you around like a dog). But they tend to have heart problems, and have trouble having babies of their own.

Lions (*Panthera leo*) and **tigers** (*Panthera tigris*) are different species in the same basic group or genus of big cats (*Panthera*). But while **ligers** may occasionally happen in the wild, they only survive in captivity. Like most cross-species hybrids, ligers are often sterile – meaning they cannot have babies of their own – and suffer from more health problems than purebred lions or tigers.

As for **elephants** and **rhinos** – they are in totally different animal families.

Though they may look a little like elephants, and they live in some of the same places, rhinos are actually more closely related to **horses** and **tapirs**. The animal families that contain elephants and rhinos split over **100 million years ago**, and have been growing apart ever since.

Elephant **tusks** are essentially super-long **teeth**, while rhino **horns** are made of hardened **hair**. Elephants are **social** (herding) animals, and rhinos are **solitary** ones. Put simply, elephants and rhinos are far too different to breed and have babies, so rhinophants will never happen. Or at least, they cannot happen naturally.

So you're saying we could make them happen? Like mix their DNA in a test tube or something?

In a way, yes. For decades now, scientists have used **genetic engineering** to make hybrid (or transgenic) animals, which contain DNA from other species. We have put **jellyfish** DNA into **mice** to make them glow in the dark, and added **mouse** DNA into **pigs**, to make them less fatty. As this technology gets more and more powerful, we may find ways of crossing animals at the DNA level, to create species the world has never seen before.

Even without genetic engineering, we have managed to produce **beefalos**, **wholphins**, and **zorses** (see next page) by cross-breeding animals in captivity. So who knows? We may one day create **catdogs**, **squabbits**, and **rhinophants**.

But then the question is: just because we **can**, does that mean we **should**? Perhaps we should focus more on protecting the animal species we already **have**, before we start trying to create crazy new ones.

Yeah. Maybe we should. Besides – that poor catdog would be *very* confused. It would probably hate itself!

CRAZY CROSS-BREEDS: HYBRID ANIMALS YOU NEVER KNEW EXISTED

Liger/Tigon

A **liger** is the offspring of a male lion and a female tiger. Ligers are **giants**, and typically weigh more than either of their parents. A **tigon** is the offspring of a male tiger and a female lion (or lioness). Tigons look more like their tiger fathers, but tend to be a little smaller.

Zorse/Zebroid

A **zorse** is a cross between a zebra and a horse. A **zebroid** is a cross between a zebra and any other equine (horse-like) species. To date, these include **zonkeys** (zebra + donkey) and **zonis** (zebra + pony). Most zebroids are dwarfs, and cannot have foals of their own.

Wholphin

This rare hybrid happens when a female bottlenose dolphin mates with a false killer whale (another type of dolphin, not actually a killer whale). Wholphins have killer-whale skin patterning, only with dark grey where the black bits would be.

Geep

The hybrid offspring of a goat and a sheep. Geeps have short, woolly coats, long, goat-like necks, and seriously cute faces. Living geeps are extremely rare, since goats and sheep have different numbers of chromosomes (gene packages) in their cells. So if you ever see one, count yourself lucky.

Cama

What do you get when you cross a camel with a llama? No, this is not a joke. It's a real animal – called a **cama**. Since camels and llamas live on different continents (Africa and America, respectively), camas do not occur in the wild. But camel-breeders in Saudi Arabia have produced many of these hybrids in captivity. Camas have the size and strength of a camel, minus the angry, stubborn personality. But their short, woolly coats make them less suited to desert travel.

ARE THERE REALLY ANY MUTANT ANIMALS AND PEOPLE?

Yes! Rather a lot of them, in fact! Mutations happen naturally, but are also created by certain types of radiation, chemicals, and bacteria. Often, mutations have no effect at all. Sometimes, they cause death and disease. But once in a while mutations can give people and animals new and unusual powers . . .

So mutation is real? There really are mutant animals and people in the world?

Mutation is totally real. But it is generally not as dramatic or exciting as it is in superhero movies. Chances are, you are some kind of mutant yourself – as were most of your human and animal ancestors.

I am? So how come I don't have any powers?

But you do! Here are just a few of them:

You can . . .

- Detect wavelengths of light that other animals cannot see! ZAP!
- Sense pressure waves in the air, and use them to identify thousands of different animals, just by the sounds they make! BOOM!
- Sense the Earth's gravitational field, and know which way is up at all times! POW!
- Picture and predict future events, using the power of your mind! BLAMMO!
- Alter your body temperature to stay warm in cold environments! WOW!

Wait a minute – those aren't powers! Everyone can do those things!

Not everyone. Plenty of animals cannot see colours, or recognize voices. Less than a quarter of them

51

can alter their internal body temperature. And very few species seem able to think, to imagine, or to guess what might happen in the future. Your other powers include speech, language recall (memory), and the ability to build fires, shelters, and Lego sets.

All of these powers and abilities, you inherited from the many generations of humans (and other animals) that came before you, with mutations happening in each generation, adding to those abilities along the way.

Two billion years ago, your ancestors could not see, hear, or do much of anything, besides ooze around and absorb things. Around **50 million years ago,** they could see, hear, climb, scuttle, hide, keep warm, and feed their young with milk made inside their own bodies. Now here you are – a mutant animal billions of years in the making, able to survive in a wide range of environments. Congratulations.

Okay, fine. I'm a mutant. So what exactly are mutations, then?

A **mutation** is **any kind of change in DNA** – the biological code inside all living cells, which tells living bodies how to grow and develop. DNA is somewhere between a blueprint and a computer program for living things. Believe it or not, every cell in your body contains all the instructions needed to build another you. Your arms, your legs, your skin, your bones, your heart, your brain – the lot. You just have to know how to read it.

A mutation is a change in that code – through certain bits of DNA getting **altered**, **deleted**, **duplicated**, or **shifted** to another part of the program. When that happens, the code is executed differently, making cells, tissues, organs, or even entire bodies develop in new and unusual ways.

So how do mutations happen?

Usually in one of three major ways:

The mutation happens naturally, or by accident. DNA has to be copied every time a cell splits into two new ones, so that every cell receives its own copy of the program. But often, that copying process creates mistakes (like typos) in the code – typos that get copied into every new cell thereafter. Often, this kind of mutation is corrected by special DNA-repair machines, which scan the DNA and fix the typos as best they can. Even when the spell-checkers miss them, these mutations are often too small to do much of anything. The code still runs the same way, and no new body parts or powers emerge. But sometimes the typo can appear in a critical part of the program, causing new effects in the host animal's body. Depending on what that effect is, it might prove helpful (like growing thick, white fur in a **snowy** environment) or harmful (like growing thick, white fur in a **desert** environment).

These kinds of mutation are typically quite small, and cause small, gradual changes in species over time. Evolution depends largely on these, and it is mostly how new species come to be.

The mutation is caused by chemicals or radiation. Here, we start to get into superhero-movie territory. DNA can be altered or damaged by certain kinds of chemical or electromagnetic radiation entering the body. This can happen to a fully grown animal or human, or it can happen to a baby in the womb.

Sadly, unlike the radioactive accidents that created Spider-Man or the Incredible Hulk, these kinds of mutations tend to hurt and damage bodies, rather than producing superpowers. Some can even kill you.

Thankfully, not all types of radiation cause mutation. Visible light, heat (infrared), and radio waves do little or no harm to our bodies at all. But **X-rays**, **gamma rays**, and **ultraviolet radiation** can all batter and mutate DNA, causing **cancer** and related diseases. This is why sunscreens and sunglasses contain chemicals to block

UV radiation, and why X-ray technicians in hospitals step out of the room before they zap you*. **Radioactive elements** like **uranium** and **plutonium** are to be avoided for the same reason.

Not all chemicals cause mutations, either. Only certain kinds of chemical, which we call **mutagens**. Some metals – like **arsenic**, **chromium**, and **nickel** – are mutagens. As are **bromine** (used to keep pools clean), **benzene** (used in glues and dyes), and **hydrogen peroxide** (used in toilet cleaners and hair-bleaching agents).

The mutation is caused by microbes. Many **viruses** – and some kinds of **bacteria** – make changes to your DNA as they hijack your cells and copy themselves. Sometimes, this does little more than make you feel tired – as with flu viruses and cold viruses. But sometimes, as with the Polio virus or Ebola virus, this can do serious damage to your body. Again, most viruses do not cause lasting mutations. But some do.

Wait – I'm confused. So do mutations cause diseases, or do they give you powers?

....

* Having a few X-rays here and there is fine, and is not harmful to the patient. But absorbing X-rays all day, every day, is not a good idea for the doctor or technician.

Most mutations do **neither** – they get fixed before they can do much damage, or are simply too small to have an effect. If a mutation does have an effect, then usually it is **not good**. Random mutations tend to **mess your code up**, creating problems, rather than new and exciting improvements.

But sometimes, very rarely, a mutation will prove helpful – giving rare abilities to the mutant animal or person that carries them.

So mutant superheroes could be real? Like the X-Men?

There are mutant people in the world with rare and unusual abilities. These are not usually as dramatic as the ones you see in superhero movies, and a few of those fictional powers – like **levitation** (flight), **invisibility**, and **laser-eyes** are simply not possible. But here are just a few of the things rare humans have been found with . . .

Super Strength!
In 2009, a 5-month-old baby in America showed strength beyond the limits of most humans, when he started doing pull-ups and other gymnastic moves in his astonished parents' arms. The little boy, **Liam Hoekstra**

was born with mutated myostatin genes, causing his muscles to grow 40% bigger than the average person.

Epic Endurance!

Finnish cross-country skiing champion **Eero Mäntyranta** competed in four Winter Olympics between 1960 and 1972, and won medals in three of them. As it turned out, he (and his entire family) had a genetic mutation that increased the oxygen-carrying capacity of his blood cells by 50%!

Unbreakable Bones!

In 1990, a middle-aged man was brought to a hospital in Connecticut, USA, after surviving a massive car crash, apparently uninjured. When doctors X-rayed him, they found he had almost unbreakable bones. This was the result of a rare mutation in his LRP5 gene, which made his bones much denser and stronger than usual.

Elastic Man!

Daniel Browning Smith (a.k.a. Rubberboy) was born with mutated collagen genes, which altered the structure of his joints, muscles, and skin. As a result, he can stretch his skin like elastic, turn his upper torso 180 degrees, and pass his entire body through a tennis racket (minus the strings).

BRAIN EVOLUTION

AMPHIBIANS

FISHES

REPTILES

HUMANS

BIRDS

MAMMALS

QUICK ONES –

GENES, MUTATIONS, AND EVOLUTION

What are genes?

Genes are coded instructions made of DNA, found in the centre of almost every cell in your body (and those of other organisms). Genes tell your cells which kinds of protein to make, and ultimately control how your body looks, moves, and behaves. Every cell contains the same set of genes – stored in huge, looping scaffolds called **chromosomes** – but different genes are switched on or off in different cell and tissue types. The total set of genes in each cell – called the **genome** – is a complete set of instructions for building another you.

Why do animals evolve?

Animals, plants, and other living things evolve over time because their environment is always changing, forcing them to adapt or die. Even within a single species, every baby animal is a little different from its parents, and from its brothers and sisters. Some are bigger and stronger, others smaller and more agile. Some are better at fighting off diseases, others better at finding mates. Whether or not a unique animal survives depends upon which ability (or **trait**) is most useful right then – in the time and place that it lives. If diseases are everywhere, the more immune ones will survive better. If food is scarce, the smaller ones may survive better (as they need less of it). If food is plentiful, the flashy ones who find more mates will survive better (or at least have more babies). Over hundreds, thousands, and millions of years, these effects combine to create change (or evolution) of a species – from scuttling rodents to flying bats, from boneless fish to tiger sharks, and from tree-dwelling apes to city-dwelling humans.

How long does it take for a new species to evolve?

New species are emerging all the time. It can take anywhere from a few months (in the case of bacteria) to tens of millions of years (in the case of mammals). Generally speaking, the faster an organism reproduces, the more rapidly a new species can evolve. The average rate of change is about a million years. But there are some periods in history – like the **Cambrian Explosion** 540 million years ago – when thousands of new species seemed to appear within a very short time. This is often the result of a huge change to the environment (such as a massive asteroid impact, or a super-volcano eruption that blankets the planet in ash for years on end), which forces everything to change fast or perish. Who knows – maybe human-caused climate change will cause another one of these explosions soon.

If humans evolved from monkeys, why are there still monkeys?

Humans did not evolve from monkeys. We evolved from the same, hairy, tree-climbing ancestor as monkeys did, but we took a different path. Monkeys stayed fairly small and became more and more adapted to living in trees. Humans grew larger, less hairy, and more and more adapted to living on open ground (in a wide range of different climates). There are still monkeys for the same reason that there are still frogs, birds, insects – all these animals have found a body shape and a way of living that works for them. As long as that holds true, they will still be around for another million years. (Hopefully, the same is true for humans.)

Does radiation make you mutate?

Yes, but usually not in a good way. Radiation is harmful to living bodies because it can pass through your skin and into your cells, smashing and breaking chemical bonds in your DNA. If that DNA was part of a gene, then that gene may be altered or deactivated, creating misshapen proteins that no longer do their job. Since proteins do all the truly clever stuff in your body – build muscles, carry oxygen, transport energy, fight infections, prevent overgrowth (cancer) – the mutations caused by radiation often cause disease. This is why scientists wear special clothing when working with radioactive materials, and why we limit our exposure to X-rays.

ATOMS, ELEMENTS, AND EXPLOSIONS

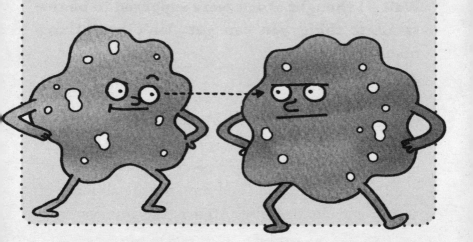

WHAT ARE ATOMS MADE OF?

Atoms are made of (even tinier) bits called protons, neutrons, and electrons. These, in turn, are made of even tinier things. Together, these are known as subatomic particles, and they form the basis of almost everything we know about matter, energy, and chemical reactions.

Wait – I thought atoms were supposed to be the smallest thing you can get. Isn't everything made of atoms?

Yes, it is. Atoms are like the Lego bricks of the physical universe. Everything you see around you is made of atoms – from the tiniest grain of sand to the tallest cliffs and skyscrapers. Oceans and deserts, rocks and rivers, plants and animals, you and me – we are all made of atoms, and nothing else. **Atoms** (like hydrogen and oxygen) combine to make **molecules** (like water, or glucose). And molecules combine to make **materials** like metal, wood, and glass. But take any material apart, and sooner or later you get down to **elements** – pure substances that cannot be broken down into simpler things – made of invisible, identical atoms.

But if we can't see them, how do we even know they're there?

Good point. In a way, they are not! Atoms are not solid, grabbable objects like Lego bricks and machine parts. They are a concept – or a model – of how our universe is built at its smallest, most basic level. The idea of the atom has actually been around for a very long time. It just took us a while to get it right, and to make it truly useful.

So who discovered atoms?

Well, the first person to talk about them was an ancient Greek scientist and philosopher called Democritus, who lived around 400 BC. Democritus was a deep thinker, and explained his idea of atoms this way:

If you split a stone in two, you get two smaller pieces of stone. Split one of those bits in half, and you get two even smaller bits. Eventually, if you keep splitting these into smaller and smaller pieces, sooner or later you will be splitting grains of sand, and eventually you will not be able to divide that little, barely visible speck any further. That smallest possible grain or particle, he called an atom (which comes from the Greek word for 'indivisible', or 'cannot be divided'). All forms of matter, said Democritus, can eventually be broken down into atoms like this. 'Nothing exists except atoms and empty space,' said Democritus. 'Everything else is opinion.'

Unfortunately, few people agreed with this idea. Back then, the ancient Greeks believed that everything was made of four basic **elements** – earth, air, fire, and water. The famous Greek philosopher Aristotle said so – and he was a lot more popular than Democritus. So everyone more or less ignored the idea of atoms, and it took more than 2,000 years for modern scientists to revisit the idea, and to build a better model of the atom.

So when did that happen?

Around 1800, the British scientist John Dalton used Democritus's idea to create his own **atomic theory**. By that time, chemistry had discovered not four, but around **20 elements**. These included common metals like **copper**, **iron**, and **lead**, rare metals like **silver**, **gold**, and **platinum**, common gases like **hydrogen** and **oxygen**, plus a few – like **soda** and **potash** which (we know now) are not really elements at all. Nevertheless, Dalton brought back the idea that **all elements are made of atoms**, and that **atoms that cannot be divided or destroyed**. In other words, the smallest lump of copper you can get is a single **atom** of copper. And the smallest amount of oxygen you can get is **one atom** of oxygen.

But didn't you say that atoms *are* made of smaller things?

They are indeed. By the early 1900s, physicists had discovered that atoms seemed to contain tiny, electrically charged particles called protons and electrons, which could be separated from each other in various ways. Later, in 1911, kiwi scientist* Ernest Rutherford drew up

* As in 'scientist born in New Zealand', not 'small, flightless bird scientist' or 'scientist who studies small, green fruit'.

67

a new model of the atom that looked more like a tiny solar system. The Rutherford Model – which chemists still use today – has a central **nucleus** of protons, with electrons orbiting around it like tiny moons. Simple atoms like hydrogen and helium have just one or two protons in their nucleus, and one or two electrons orbiting around it. More complex atoms like carbon and copper have a cluster of protons in the middle, and a cloud of electrons whizzing around them.

Twenty years after Rutherford created this updated model of the atoms, we discovered another subatomic particle called a **neutron**, which has no electrical charge[*] at all, and clusters in the nucleus alongside the protons.

So we had to redraw the atom all over again?

Right. Although the idea of atoms began in ancient Greece, we only really figured out how they are put together – and how they work – within the last century. With every new discovery in physics, we have had to look again at what we think atoms actually are.

And it gets weirder. Around 1960, we discovered that protons, neutrons, and electrons are made of even tinier particles called **quarks**.

---

[*] Hence the name – neutron, meaning 'thing with a neutral charge'.

Wait – what?

Yep – quarks. There are six **flavours** of quark (up, down, strange, charmed, top, and bottom), and quarks are stuck together by **gluons** to create **protons** and **neutrons** (an **electron** is just a single quark, in one particular flavour).

So what holds the protons and neutrons together?

An impossibly strong force which is 100 times stronger than electromagnetism, and trillions of times stronger than gravity. It is called – imaginatively – the **strong nuclear force.**

This force makes it incredibly difficult to break the nucleus of an atom into pieces. But as we discovered in 1938, it can be done. This is called **nuclear fission**.

If you can get it to go fast enough, you can fire a free neutron straight at a nucleus and smash it into bits, releasing neutrons from the nucleus (along with a good amount of energy).

Some of those freed neutrons may then smash into the nuclei of other, nearby atoms, smashing them to bits, and releasing more free neutrons and energy. If you can make this happen enough times in a large enough lump of material, then you can create a nuclear chain reaction that releases an enormous amount of light, heat, and energy.

Left to run out of control, this might lead to a catastrophic **nuclear explosion**. This is, in fact, how nuclear bombs and missiles work. But if you can harness and control that chain reaction, you can convert the steady supply of energy it releases into heat, light, or electrical power. This is exactly what happens inside a nuclear power plant.

So let me get this straight: everything is made of atoms . . .

Right.

. . . atoms have mad energy . . .

Yep.

. . . and you can use atoms to power a whole city – or to blow it up?

Bingo. The atom is a truly powerful idea. Once you understand how atoms work, you can understand pretty much all the physical sciences. Then you can buy yourself a T-shirt that says: **I'm not scared of physics and chemistry – let me atom**.

Groan!

Hehe. Sorry.

WHAT DO ATOMS AND PARTICLES ACTUALLY LOOK LIKE?

Atoms are far too small to see with the naked eye, and even the world's most powerful electron microscopes can barely pick out an atomic nucleus as a vague dot or blob. The particles (protons and neutrons) inside the nucleus are even tinier, and we have yet to get a clear look at any of those. As for electrons and quarks – they are so tiny as to be practically invisible.

But using mathematics, we can predict what shape a proton might be, based on which kinds of quarks are inside it and how fast they jostle around. As it turns out, not all particles are little balls or spheres.

Here are four shapes we think might exist, if only we could see them:

Sphere – protons containing slower, lower-energy quarks take this shape

Bagel – the shape created when speedy quarks spin the opposite direction from their parent proton

Rugby Ball – made by slower-moving quarks moving in the same pattern as bagels

Peanut – made when speedy quarks spin the same way as the overall proton

WHY DO ALL THE ELEMENTS HAVE THEIR OWN LITTLE LETTERS AND NUMBERS?

Some time ago, chemists began arranging chemical elements into one, huge table called the Periodic Table. Each element in the table has its own code letter (or letters) so that you can squeeze 100 or more of them into one table. And the numbers tell you how heavy each element is, and what their atoms look like.

So the letters are basically just initials? Like, I'm SM (Sean Murphy), so oxygen is just Mr O?

That's one way to think about it, yes. Oxygen is Mr O, nitrogen is Mr N, and sulphur is Mr S!

Periodic Table of the Elements

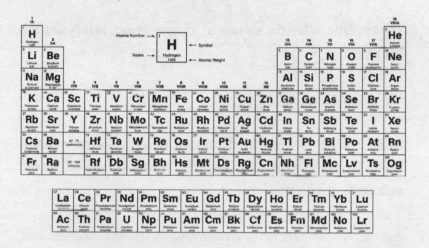

Then why do some elements have more than one letter?

Well, there are over 118 known elements, and we only have 26 letters in the alphabet.

So quite simply, there are not enough single letters to go around. Also, many elements start with the same letter, which would give them the same initial if you only used one. For example, phosphorus, platinum, polonium, palladium, and plutonium all begin with P. Of these, phosphorus was discovered and named first. So phosphorus gets to be just P, while the others are given the symbols Pt, Po, Pd, and Pu. That way, we can still tell which one is which.

Okay, but why do some of them start with weird letters?

How d'you mean?

Like, gold is Au, and silver is Ag. Why aren't they just Go and Si instead? Were those already taken?

Actually, no. There is no element with the symbol Go, and although **silicon** has taken the symbol **Si**, we discovered and named silver long before we got around to silicon.

So then why Ag? There isn't even an 'a' or a 'g' in silver!

Because not all the elements have symbols based on their names in English. Some – like silver and gold – are based their names in Latin. In Latin, silver is *argentum*, and gold is *aurum*. Hence, **Ag** and **Au**. The Latin word for lead is *plumbium*, and the word for mercury is *hydragyrum* (which literally means 'water silver'). Which is why lead has the symbol **Pb**, and mercury is **Hg**.

In the early days of science and chemistry, many scientists wrote and published their findings in Latin, so that English, Italian, Swedish, and German scientists could all use the same language. Which is why there are so many symbols based on Latin names. But a few elements have symbols based on their names in Greek, German, or other languages. The symbol for **iron (Fe)** comes from its Greek name, *ferrum*, and **tungsten** has the symbol **W** because it was discovered by German chemists – who called it *wolfram*.

Ah – I get it. What about the numbers, then? What are they for?

The numbers above and below the symbol of each element tell you how heavy or light its atom is, relative to other elements, and what the atom of that element looks like. If you read the table like a comic strip – the boxes from left to right, and rows from top to bottom – then the elements get more massive the further across and down you go. The number above each symbol is called the

atomic number. This is a kind of rank order of elements, with #1 (**hydrogen**) being the first and lightest, and #118 (**oganmesson**) the last and heaviest known element.

What about the number underneath?

That one is called the **atomic mass**. It tells you how heavy one atom of each element is. This includes the weight of the **nucleus**, plus the **electrons** orbiting around it. But since electrons weigh next to nothing, it basically tells you the total weight of protons and neutrons in the nucleus.

Since atoms are so tiny and light, you cannot measure this in kilograms (kg), grams (g) or even micrograms (µg) – millionths of a gram. So instead, the weight is given in atomic mass units (amu or u). One gram is equal to roughly 1.7 octillion atomic mass units[*]. Hydrogen – with just one proton in its nucleus – weighs just 1u. The nucleus of an iron atom has 26 protons and 30 neutrons, and an atomic mass of roughly 56u (26+30 – see how that works?). Even the heaviest elements – like uranium and plutonium – only have atomic masses of 200 or so. In other words, an iron atom is about 50 times heavier than a hydrogen atom, and a uranium atom is about 4

....

[*] While a million is a 1 with six zeros after it (1,000,000), an octillion is a 1 with 27 zeros after it (1,000,000,000,000,000,000,000,000,000)!

times heavier than an iron atom, and 200 times heavier than a hydrogen one.

Is that why iron is a solid, heavy metal, and hydrogen is a light, floaty gas?

That's part of it, yes. But how an element looks and behaves depends only partly on its mass (or weight), but mostly on how 'friendly' it is with other atoms. We'll talk more about that later on.

Fair enough. One last thing – why bother putting all the elements into a table in the first place? Is it just so we don't accidentally forget one of them – like making a shopping list?

Not quite, but close. The Periodic Table is a bit more than just a simple checklist. It is actually a kind of **blueprint** for how elements act and behave in the wild. It contains groups of elements with similar traits – with metals grouped in the left and middle, non-metals and gases grouped on the right.

One group of elements is **highly reactive** (even explosive!), while another **barely reacts at all**. One group contains **hard**, **shiny metals**, and another one **soft**, **brittle powders**. To a trained chemist, one look at the table can reveal tonnes of information about any given element.

And in a way, the Periodic Table is like a shopping list, since scientists have used it to predict the existence of new and undiscovered elements – even using it to create new elements, artificially. In fact, everything to the right of uranium (atomic number 92) on the table is a synthetic element – one created in the laboratory by scientists, rather than found naturally. Some of these – like **flevorium** – exist for less than a second before spontaneously splitting into smaller atoms of another element!

An element that self-destructs in less than a second? What's the point in that?

Well, if nothing else it's a good way to win a Nobel Prize in Chemistry, which gets you a real gold medal and roughly a million euros (or dollars) in cash . . .

What?! Okay – now where did I put my chemistry set . . .

THE 10 RAREST ELEMENTS ON THE PLANET

Some elements – like carbon, iron, and oxygen – are found everywhere on Earth, and there are billions of tonnes of them altogether. Others are much rarer, and only a few kilograms – or even a few grams – of them are found or created each year.

Here are the top 10 rarest elements on Earth, in descending order:

ELEMENT	SYMBOL	ATOMIC MASS
ASTATINE	At	210
OGANESSON	Og	294
BERKELIUM	Bk	247
FRANCIUM	Fr	223
PROTACTINIUM	Pa	231
PROMETHIUM	Pm	145
CALIFORNIUM	Cf	251
AMERICIUM	Am	243
CURIUM	Cm	247
NEPTUNIUM	Np	237

IS THERE AN ACID THAT CAN DISSOLVE EVERYTHING?

Some strong acids can eat through flesh, bone, metal, glass, or plastic.

But an acid's ability to dissolve things depends upon specific chemical reactions. Because of this, no one type of acid can eat through everything. At least none we have made or discovered yet.

So why do acids eat things? How do they work?

Acids are complex chemicals that eat through (or **corrode**) other materials on contact. They do this by donating charged atoms (called **ions**) to the thing they are dissolving. As these ions meet the surface of the material, they react with the atoms therein – breaking chemical bonds, stealing free atoms, and rearranging the structure as they go. In this way, a strong acid can eat right through a piece of metal or glass. Or at the very least, leave a serious dent.

Yikes! That sounds pretty scary.

Acids can be scary. But happily, most acids are rather boring and mild, and cannot eat through much of anything. In fact, fruit juice, vinegar, and fizzy drinks all contain acids, which do us no harm at all in moderation.

There's acid in fruit juice?

Yep. **Citrus fruits** like oranges, lemons, and limes all contain citric acid – which is part of what gives them that satisfying, sour taste. Actually, pretty much everything that tastes sour to us contains an acid of some kind, as the **taste buds** that detect sour tastes are basically just acid-detectors. **Vinegar** and **tomato ketchup** taste sour because they contain **acetic** or **ethanoic** acid. And the pleasing 'bite' you get from **fizzy drinks**? That comes from the **carbonic acid** dissolved within.

And those acids don't hurt us at all?

For the most part, no. The citric, acetic, and carbonic acids you find in these foods are too weak to burn or damage our insides. These acids can eat into the surface of your teeth. So if you drink fruit juice and fizzy drinks all the time, then you might end up with more cavities and trips to the dentist for fillings. But by the time they hit your stomach, they are little threat to you at all. In fact, your stomach contains powerful, concentrated acids that dissolve your food into mush during digestion! The **hydrochloric acid** in your stomach is almost as corrosive as battery acid, and can damage teeth, bones, and other tissues when it leaks or splashes out.

So what stops your stomach acid from eating right through you?

Firstly, a fatty protective **lining** to the stomach, which the acid has trouble reacting with. As long as this lining stays intact, you are fine*. And to protect the rest of your digestive system, your body makes special chemicals called alkalis (or bases), which get mixed with the acidic

....

* Although sometimes, when this lining gets damaged by bacteria, acids can eat into the stomach walls, creating **stomach ulcers**. Nasty, painful business, those.

food-slush before it is passed to the intestines. This deactivates the acid, and renders it harmless.

Cool. How does it do that?

Bases are like the dark twins of acids. Where acids contain lots of free **positive ions**, bases contain free **negative ions**. These negative ions can eat through things, too, and can be very corrosive when they react with bare skin. But when they are added to acids, the negative ions bind to the positive ones, cancelling (or neutralizing) them.

Bases and alkalis can be handy. Since they damage and dissolve bacteria, you can find them in **bleaches**, **bathroom cleaners**, and dissolved (in safe amounts) in **hot tubs** and **swimming pools**. You also find them in baking soda and food marinades.

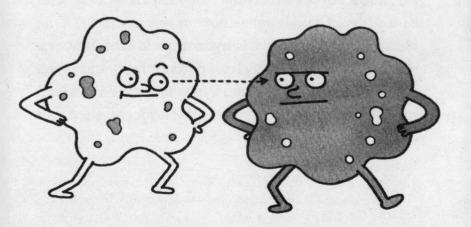

Hmmm – seems like acids aren't so bad after all.

Well, some types of acid are da\ngerous. Some – like sulphuric acid – not only eat into your skin, they also release massive amounts of heat as they react with the water in living tissues – creating smouldering acid burns that are nobody's idea of a good time. These are especially dangerous when they get in your eyes, where they react with watery tissues and tear ducts and create severe burns and **blindness**. For this reason, chemists always wear eye protection when working with strong acids, and you should never – and I mean never – squirt household cleaners anywhere near your face.

Most acids will not dissolve metals like gold and platinum, which have stable arrangements of atoms that resist invasion by those free ions in acids. But some like **aqua regia** (a mixture of two acids – nitric and hydrochloric) can dissolve more or less any metal. One of the nastiest, perhaps, is **hydrofluoric acid**. That one will eat through metal, glass, pottery, flesh and bone. Spill a whole cup of that stuff in your lap, and it would eat right through your legs. So some acids really are that bad!

But if it eats through everything, how do they even store that stuff and move it around? Wouldn't it just eat through whatever you were keeping it in?

Happily, even hydrofluoric acid cannot eat through some types of plastic. Plastic polymers have chemical bonds that repel water, making it hard for the acid to get a toehold on the surface and start a reaction. So chemists and factory workers can store these dangerous acids in thick, plastic barrels, and protect against acid burns with thick plastic gloves and glasses. But if you ever see a sign like the one below on a bottle or a barrel, then **do not mess with it**. Trust me – whatever's in there, you don't want to get it on ya . . .

Right! Got it!

ACIDS (AND BASES) IN EVERYDAY LIFE

While acids and bases are dangerous, and others downright scary, others come in handy for cooking, cleaning, and other household uses. Here are a few you might find in your kitchen, your bathroom, or in the cupboard under the sink:

Baking Soda

Technically known as sodium bicarbonate. Mostly used for baking, as it reacts with certain ingredients to release carbon dioxide, helping cakes to rise. But when mixed into a paste, it can also work as a mouthwash, a carpet stain remover, or a neutralizer for insect bites and bee stings!

Soap

Many soaps are made by mixing animal or vegetable fats with strong bases like potassium or sodium hydroxide –

often from solutions of wood ash (or lye). As such, these fatty or oily bases help clean surfaces and disinfect skin when safely diluted with water. Soaps can also make a powerful insect repellant.

Vinegar

Vinegars are acidic, and depending on what they are made from, they may contain varying amounts of acetic, citric, or tartaric acid. Mostly used for flavouring and pickling foods (most bacteria cannot grow in acidic environments, which is why pickled foods can be stored for so long without spoiling). But it can also be used as a (rather stinky) house cleaner or weed killer.

Citric Acid

Often added to foods as a preservative, but can be found naturally in citrus fruits like oranges, lemons, and limes. When diluted, can also be used to clean things.

Toothpaste

Most toothpastes are weak bases (as acids corrode the surface of your teeth), and keep your teeth and gums free of bacteria by creating an unwelcome environment. Toothpastes can also work well on stings and insect bites – neutralizing the itchy, burning acids inside.

HOW DO POWER PLANTS MAKE ENERGY?

Power plants do not really make energy. Rather, they convert one form of energy to another, more convenient one. Conventional power plants release chemical energy stored in fuels and turn them into electrical power. But renewable energy plants capture and transform energy from moving wind, falling water, or the core of the Earth itself!

Wait – if power plants don't make energy, then where does energy come from?

One of the first and most important laws of physics is this: **energy can neither be created, nor destroyed.** All the energy in the universe was actually created at the moment of the Big Bang. Ever since then, that energy has just been **transferred** from one place to another, and **recycled** from one form to another. Light, heat, electricity, and movement are all forms of energy, and can be converted from one form to another. And this is happening all the time, whether you realize it or not.

I don't get it.

Okay – then try this: place your palms together, and rub them really hard and fast for about 20 seconds. What happens?

They get hot. And I get tired.

Right. So what you did there was use **movement** to produce **heat**. You transformed one form of energy into another, using **friction** (the force of resistance between two materials rubbing together). But you did not do it for free. You got tired, because it took **energy** to produce that rubbing movement in the first place. This was **chemical energy** stored in your body, which you converted into movement using your muscles.

Hmmm – so where did *I* get the chemical energy from?

From food! Food – whether from plants or from animals – contains stored chemical energy, too. Where did that energy come from, you ask? Well, follow the food chain far enough, and you get to . . .

The sun?

Exactly. The sun got its energy from the Big Bang*. Plants capture sunlight and convert it into chemical energy. Animals (including humans) eat that energy, and use it to move, heat, and power our bodies. And so it goes.

But food is not the only form of energy we humans like to use. Since prehistoric times, we have burned **wood** to make fires – converting the **chemical energy** stored in dead trees into **heat** and **light**. Since ancient Roman times, we have mined and burned **coal** for the same purpose. For hundreds of years, we have collected, purified, and burned **oil** (petroleum) and **natural gas** to provide fuel for lamps, heaters (chemical energy into light and heat), and for factory engines, motor cars, and aeroplanes (chemical energy into movement). In short, we humans are masters of energy conversion. And we show no signs of stopping.

....

* It took several billion years for that energy to make its way from the Big Bang into the formation of our sun – but that's another, much longer, story.

What about power plants? They don't make heat and light. They make electricity.

Right you are. Modern power plants use all kinds of different energy sources – including fossil fuels like coal and gas, or renewable sources like biomass and geothermal energy. But the goal is always the same – to turn the energy trapped in fuels or natural systems into another form that we can **store** in batteries, and **transmit** through cables to our houses – **electricity**.

So how do they do it?

Most of them do it using **generators**. A **generator** is any machine that converts **mechanical energy** (or **movement**) into **electrical energy** or **power**.

There are a few different types of generator, but all of them use the same basic idea: stick some magnets on an axle, make it spin, and the magnet will push and pull at metal objects in an alternating pattern. If you place that spinning magnet inside a coil of metal wire, then tiny **electrical charges** will start to flow back and forth inside that wire. Attach that wire to a lightbulb, a heater, or any other electrical gadget, and the **electrical current** will power that gadget. Bingo – you just generated electricity from movement, using

electromagnetic induction. British physicist Michael Faraday first discovered how to do this in 1831, and engineers have been using induction to generate electricity (on larger and larger scales) ever since.

Of course, it still takes energy – in the form of **movement** – to spin or rotate the coil. You can make this movement in various ways.

The simplest way is to turn a handle attached to the spinning coil by hand. This is called a hand-crank generator, and you can actually buy them to charge electric camping lights and smartphones.

Does that really work?

It really does. But it's not much fun. And there is a limit to how much electrical power you can produce this way.

Electrical power is measured in units called watts. The average person can generate about 10-50 W (watts) of electrical power on a hand crank. If you crank away at a hand-powered generator for 1 minute, you will convert enough movement into electricity to power a 10-watt LED lightbulb for about 10 minutes. To keep the light on for an hour, you would have to crank away for 5 or 6 minutes straight. Charging a smartphone takes a bit longer – roughly 10 minutes of cranking for an hour or so of charge.

That doesn't sound so bad. What about if you tried to heat your house like that?

Well, depending on how big your house is – and how cold it is outside – it takes between **10** and **50 kW** (**kilowatts**) of power to heat a house. That's a thousand times more power than you need to light a lightbulb. So to heat a whole house for just 2 hours, you would need to crank away on the generator for roughly **200 hours**. Or eight days straight, 24 hours per day, without stopping to eat or sleep.

Urgh. Not fun. What about charging an electric car, like a Tesla?

Electric car batteries need about **50–100 kW** of power. So again, you would have to crank all day, every day, for **1–2 weeks**, just to get one full battery charge in your Tesla*.

Really doesn't seem worth it, does it?

Not at all. Which is why power plants do not contain hundreds of people cranking away at hand-turned

---

* In practice, you could not supply the charge quickly enough to charge a Tesla battery at all. But we'll ignore that for the moment.

generators. Far better to get something else to turn the handle for you. And that something is called a **turbine**.

Turbines are like propellors in reverse. Propellors turn stored energy (petrol or electricity) into movement in the propellor's blades – driving a boat through the water, or an aeroplane through the gassy air. Turbines work the other way around. **Fast-moving water** or **gas** pushes against the blades of the turbine, creating movement in the shaft it is mounted on. That spinning shaft spins the axle of the generator, converting movement into electricity just like the hand-crank does (only much, much faster).

WIND/
WATER/
STEAM

ELECTRICITY

So where do you get the moving water or gas from?

Good question. That depends on the type of power plant. **Hydro-electric power plants** are built on dams, from which water falls through tubes right onto the turbines.

In **wind-power facilities** (or **wind farms**), the generators are mounted on the heads of giant **wind turbines**. Wind turns the sails (or **rotors**), and the rotors spin the axle of the generator behind. The only problem with these is that you need a hefty river to build one upon, and damming those rivers can create problems for wildlife and human communities nearby.

Conventional power plants drive their turbines in a different way. Inside these plants, **coal**, **gas**, or **oil** is burned to create heat, and that heat is transferred to huge tanks of water, creating jets of superheated, fast-moving steam. The steam rushes past the blades of the turbines, spinning their turbines, providing movement for the electrical generator.

But burning coal and oil pollutes the atmosphere, doesn't it? Isn't that why we have global warming and stuff?

That's a big part of it, yes. Plus coal, gas, and oil are in a limited supply, and we will eventually run out (or at least, the remaining pockets of it will be so hard to get at, that it will take more energy to extract them than we actually get out of processing them).

Geothermal power plants get around both of these problems by using a clean, unlimited energy source to heat water and drive their turbines. Namely, the hot, molten interior of the planet itself! By digging holes and placing water pipes into underground heat wells, they can boil water using the natural heat of the planet alone, sometimes providing enough power for an entire city.

Whoa! So why can't we all just use *that*?

Well, geothermal plants have to be built in places where the Earth's crust is thinner, or where hot pockets of water and molten rock lie closer to the surface. Places like Iceland and the Philippines have lots of these. In other places, you would have to dig so deep to get at the heat source that right now it is just not worth the effort.

What about nuclear power?

Nuclear power uses a different energy source, but the same, basic pathway to producing electricity. Inside a nuclear reactor's core, atoms of **uranium** are split, releasing the immense energy stored in the nucleus of each one. With enough uranium – and plenty of safety measures in place – this creates a controlled chain-reaction, and a steady supply of energy and heat. That heat is then used to superheat water and power steam-driven turbines and generators – just as you might find in a coal- or gas-fired plant.

Unlike fossil fuels, nuclear fuel does not create carbon dioxide or other harmful waste gases, so nuclear power plants are generally better for the environment than coal, gas, or oil ones. But nuclear fuels are difficult to handle safely, and they do create **solid**, **radioactive wastes**, which can remain a danger to plants and animals for hundreds or thousands of years! So we have to be careful where we store those wastes – usually burying them in radiation-absorbing containers, deep below the ground.

Yeesh. Seems like every kind of power plant has its problems.

You're right – most do. But maybe some day we will figure it all out!

WE'VE GOT THE POWER!

We humans love our electricity and power, and have more than a few ways of generating it.

Fossil Fuels – 64%

Coal, oil, and natural gas are all forms of fossil fuel – burned in power plants to release thousands of years' worth of stored energy inside. Right now, we generate most of our electricity this way. Unfortunately, burning fossil fuels also releases trillions of tonnes of carbon dioxide into the atmosphere, contributing to climate change and other environmental problems.

Hydro-electric Power – 16%

Hydro-electric plants harness the gravitational force contained within huge volumes of falling water, and are typically built by damming large rivers to create a kind of artificial waterfall. Hydropower plants release few wastes or pollutants, but building them can be expensive and harmful to local plants, animals, and human communities.

Nuclear Power – 10%

Nuclear power first arrived in the 1950s, when we learned to harness the energy inside radioactive elements like uranium and plutonium. Although a low-carbon energy source, the radioactive waste products of nuclear energy still pose a problem, as they can emit harmful radiation for hundreds or thousands of years.

Wind Power – 5%

Wind farms and individual wind turbines supply a huge amount of energy to parts of Europe, Asia, and the Americas. Some are built on windy plains and hilltops, others in massive offshore clusters. Although clean and renewable, wind turbines can be unreliable in less windy climates, and some people simply do not like like looking at them.

Solar Power – 2%

Solar farms and power plants convert energy from the sun into usable heat or electricity, in a clean, reliable, and increasingly efficient way. The use of solar power is growing steadily, but for now is still limited by the high cost of solar panels, reflectors, and roof tiles.

Geothermal Power – <1%

Geothermal plants harness energy trapped in hot rocks and water pockets beneath the ground – using that heat to create steam to drive turbines. Though generally non-polluting and environmentally friendly, they cannot be built everywhere, and have more limited use in many places.

Biomass Power – <1%

Wood, paper, and energy-rich peats can all be burned to create heat and light. Some plants can also be harvested and processed to create biofuels to power cars and households. A few countries also burn animal poo to create electricity, in special biomass power plants! In all, though, biomass power is only a small part of our total energy generation worldwide.

Wave/Tidal Power – <1%

Wave and tidal power use the rocking, sloshing motions of waves and tides – in effect converting wind movement and gravitational energy into electricity. Though promising, only a tiny fraction of the world's power is currently made this way.

WHY CAN'T WE JUST GET ALL OUR POWER FROM THE SUN?

Solar energy is clean, renewable, and practically unlimited. In some places, it is already being used to supply entire households, villages, and towns. But capturing enough solar power to meet the needs of an entire country – or even the world – is something we have yet to figure out.

So we *could* power the whole world with solar power? We just can't do it *yet*?

Right. The sun supplies more energy than we humans could ever need. Just one hour of sunlight contains over **430 quintillion (430,000,000,000,000,000,000) joules** of energy. The total amount of energy used by every human on the planet is around 410 quintillion joules. In other words, one hour's worth of sunlight could power our entire planet for a year – if only we could capture and store all of it.

So why can't we capture it all now?

There are actually a few different reasons for that. Firstly, compared with other forms of electricity production, solar power production is pretty leaky.

Unlike coal, gas, oil, nuclear, and geothermal plants, most **solar power plants** do not use their energy source to heat water and drive turbines and generators. Instead, the energy from solar radiation (sunlight) is converted directly into electricity, using **solar cells**. The cells are made with special **photoelectric materials** – metals that release tiny electrical charges when they are struck by sunlight. When a beam of light hits a metal like this, tiny charged particles (**electrons**) are knocked loose from the metal atoms at the surface. If you arrange thin sheets of those metals just right, then electrons will start to flow from one layer to another, building up an **electrical charge** inside. The charge inside any one solar cell is pretty feeble. But if you wire enough solar cells together, you get enough electricity to light and heat a house, a factory, or even an entire town!

So what's the problem?

The problem is not all of that sunlight gets 'harvested'. When sunlight hits a solar cell, some of it bounces off, some of it goes straight through, and some of it is absorbed. Only the sunlight that gets absorbed can be converted into electricity, and even then, some energy is lost to heat in the process. In all, solar cells can only capture and convert around **20% (or one fifth)** of the sunlight that hits them. Meaning most of the energy from the sunlight goes unused.

But there's another problem, too . . .

Like, how do you make solar power at night?

Right – you can't. Once the sun goes down, there is no sunlight to convert. Of course, if you live in the desert or in the tropics, you can still capture sunlight and turn it into electricity all day long, and most of the year round. Then you can store and use that energy by night. There are already solar-powered homes in Australia, the Middle East, and the Mediterranean that get most or all of their power this way, with roofs and garden spaces covered in solar panels. Some produce more electricity than they use, and share the excess with other houses nearby, as part of a local power grid.

But what if you live somewhere dark and cloudy, like Scotland or Iceland or something?

Good point. Darker places further from the equator may have plenty of wind power (in the case of Scotland), or geothermal energy (in the case of Iceland). But they simply do not receive enough hours of sunlight each day to power a home with solar energy – let alone an entire town.

This is one of the reasons why solar energy has really taken off in some places, but remains rare in others. Worldwide, we get less than 5% of our energy from renewable sources, and less than half of *that* is from solar energy sources*. But as the technology continues to get better and cheaper, we will likely see solar power everywhere it can be in the world, while the darker, cloudier places turn to other forms of renewable energy.

That said, one day, we may get around this problem in another way – by building solar power plants in **space**.

What? Can we even do that?

In some ways, we already are. Our satellites and space stations already run on solar power, though they rarely collect more than they use themselves. One idea is that we could build massive solar panels and batteries in an armada of solar satellites, then beam that stored energy down to Earth in the form of **microwaves**.

Capturing solar energy in space has some huge advantages, as more than half of the energy in sunlight is lost as it gets bounced and reflected by the Earth's atmosphere. If you can capture sunlight outside the

* Compare that with 40% from coal, 20% from natural gas, 16% from hydro-electric energy, and 10% from nuclear.

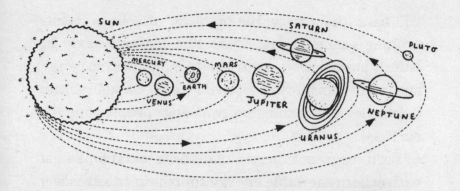

atmosphere, you get twice as much energy for your efforts.

One crazy idea is to create an immense, ball-like cage of solar cells **around the sun itself**. The structure – called a **Dyson sphere** – would let plenty of sunlight through, but being so close to the sun, it could capture a nearly unlimited supply of energy. Enough to power our planet for thousands of years, and perhaps enough to fuel super-fast spacecraft that could travel between solar systems, even to other galaxies.

That. Sounds. Awesome.

It does, doesn't it? Unfortunately – for now, at least – the Dyson sphere is still just an idea. We cannot actually build one with current spacecraft and materials. And while China, Japan, and the UK are all working on Space-Based Solar Power (SBSP) technologies, we still have to overcome the problems of how to get the orbiting generators up there (too big and heavy to launch in one piece, too tricky to build them in orbit), and with transmitting stored energy back to Earth (without accidentally microwaving people on the surface!).

So in the meantime, we might have to combine solar with **other renewable energy sources** in order to meet the global need for electricity.

Every place has some sort of renewable energy it can already use. Solar energy in the deserts and tropics. Wind and wave energy on the coasts. Hydro-electric energy in the mountains.

And even without Dyson spheres and other futuristic technologies, scientists say we could use the sources and technologies that **we already have** to make the world 100% powered by renewable energy by the year 2050. We just need to commit to doing it.

So what are we waiting for?

Yup – let's do it!

TRY IT YOURSELF: CAPTURE THE SUN, BUILD A NIGHTLIGHT

Harness the power of the sun by day, and use that energy at night, by making a solar-powered nightlight with a few simple materials.

You will need:

- 2 glass jam jars
- 2 solar-powered lights

The lights are those little ones you can buy to light up garden paths. The round top should fit just inside the mouth of the jar.

Take the tops off both jam jars and set them aside.

Twist the solar path lights apart, separating the top from the base.

Remove the paper strip protecting the battery.

Check that the tops of the path lights (with the solar panels) fit snugly inside the rim of the jam jars.

Set the solar panel tops in the sun for a full day.

Use your solar-powered lanterns to read more of this book in bed!

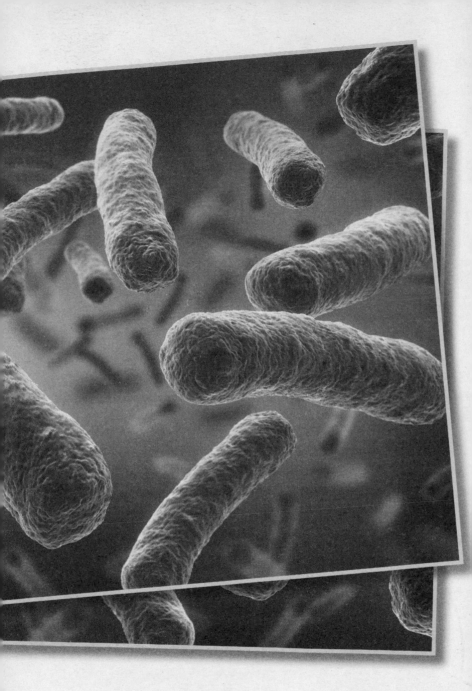

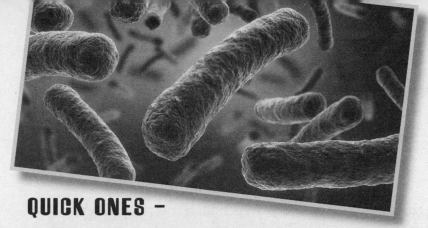

QUICK ONES –
ATOMS, ELEMENTS, AND EXPLOSIONS

Is there a microscope that can see atoms?

Sort of, yes. Although atoms are too small for even the most powerful light microscopes to pick out, scanning electron microscopes have been used to create images of large metallic atoms (like iron and palladium atoms) locked into cage-like patterns. Even these are pretty blob-like and blurry, and nobody has managed a picture of a single, tiny hydrogen or helium atom. Maybe one day

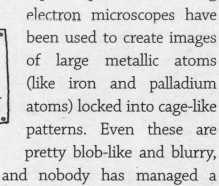

we will do better. But for now, we are stuck with the limits of our microscope technology.

Would other planets have the same elements as ours?

As far as we know, yes. Although it is possible there may be some as-yet-unknown elements lurking somewhere out there in the universe, we have already discovered most or all of the elements we think are possible. In other words, elements that result from known combinations of protons, neutrons, and electrons, in patterns stable enough to occur naturally (and hang around more than a millisecond). We have already discovered the lightest and heaviest elements possible. So for a 'new' element to exist, it would have to be found in the gaps between known elements, built of subatomic particles we have yet to discover. Chances are, that won't happen, and all elements – everywhere – will be the same.

Why do only some things burn and explode?

Burning and exploding are types of chemical reaction, and – thankfully – not all chemical elements or compounds (mixtures of elements) can be made to react in this way. When a substance burns or explodes, it is **reacting** with the air around it, spurred on by the addition of a heat source (like a match or electrical spark). Some substances (like wood, rubber, and petrol) react very easily to heat and oxygen. Others (like water and steel) cannot be made to, no matter how hard you try. Nuclear explosions are a little different . . .

What makes nuclear bombs so powerful?

Nuclear bombs harness the immense energy contained within the nucleus of an atom, by smashing or splitting atomic nuclei to break the bonds between particles (protons and neutrons) inside. A single split or smashed atom only releases a small amount of energy. But with the right type of material – and the right kind of explosive trigger – a nuclear chain reaction is created, releasing massive amounts of energy from trillions of splitting or fusing atoms – all at the same time. This creates an immense amount of heat, and a crushing wave of air pressure, which can combine to destroy an entire city in seconds. Thankfully, nuclear bombs have only been used twice in the history of the world, during World War Two. Let's hope we never see them used again.

How do you make petrol?

Petrol (or gasoline) is made from crude oil, which is pumped from deep, underground pockets using massive drills and oil rigs. From there, the crude oil is shipped to a refinery, where it is heated and boiled to separate the energy-rich molecules (called hydrocarbons) inside. Gases drawn from different parts of the tall, column-like boiling chamber contain different types of hydrocarbons, and are collected and purified to make different types of fuel. These include gasoline (petrol), kerosene, and diesel oil. From there, the various fuel types are shipped, piped, or trucked from the refinery to petrol stations, where people fill up their cars, lorries, and motorbikes.

PLANTS, HABITAT, AND CLIMATE

HOW DO PLANTS KNOW WHERE TO GROW?

Plants may seem pretty simple and stupid. But they are actually complex life-forms with keen senses, clever strategies, and a remarkable ability to adapt. They can sense gravity and sunlight, feel their way around objects by touch, and figure out where, when, and how much to grow. But this all happens so slowly that we hardly ever notice it.

Come on, plants aren't clever. They can't think or move or anything. They just sit there and soak up sunshine, don't they?

Plants may not have brains or legs, but they are smarter than you think. And they move quite a lot. They just do it so slowly that we fast-paced animals barely notice it.

Animals move on the scale of **seconds** or **minutes**, so it is easy to see them in motion. Plants move on the scale of **hours**, **days**, and **weeks**, so it is much harder to spot them at it. Trying to catch plants moving and growing is like staring at the minute or hour hands on a clock. We know the hands are moving, but our eyes and brains cannot register movement that slow. So it looks like they are not moving at all.

There are exceptions to these rules, though. Some animals, like sponges and anemones, barely move at all and appear more like plants. While some plants, like the **Venus flytrap,** and the **sensitive plant** move in seconds, or fractions of a second. Sensitive plants fold their leaves in seconds when touched, while Venus flytraps snap their jaw-like leaves shut when insects touch the **trigger hairs** upon them.

Cool! But if most plants move too slowly to see, then how do we know they're moving at all?

Well, if you were to peek at a clock once or twice an hour, you would see the minute and hour hands had moved quite a lot in between. If you were to take photographs once a minute during this time, then you could assemble a whole day's worth of snapshots and play them back like an animated movie. What would you see then?

I suppose . . . the minute hand would be spinning round really fast, and the hour hand would slowly do a full circle?

Right*. Now imagine you did that with a growing **sunflower** – taking snapshots every minute, and compiling them into a stop motion movie. What would you see then?

I dunno. Maybe they grow a bit upwards?

Probably, yes. But you would also see them turn to face the sun, tracking it across the sky from east to west each day.

They do that?

Yep. When growing sunflowers feel that sun on their leaves, it triggers the release of **hormones** inside the plant, which make it twist and bend (in the direction of the most strongly sunlit leaves). As the sun arcs across the sky the flower continues to twist and track the sun, angling its leaves and petals towards it like a satellite dish.

　This kind of **light-sensing** movement in plants is

．．．

* Actually if you did it for a whole day (24 hours), then the hour hand would spin through two full circles, but you get the idea.

called **phototropism**, and lots of plants do it, in lots of different ways. Many plants **unfurl** their leaves and petals by day, and **curl them** up by night, as if packing them away. **Plant stems** grow towards sunlight, while **plant roots** grow away from it. This is one way that plants can orientate themselves, and move through their environment. But light is not the **only** trigger for plant movement. Many plants can not only **see** where they grow. They can **smell**, **taste**, and **feel** their way around, also.

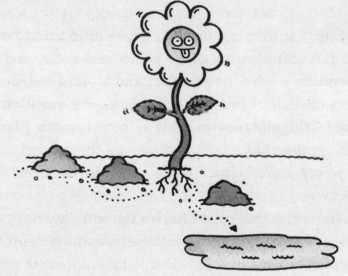

Wait – plants can feel things, too?

Yep. They not only sense and respond to light (**phototropism**). They can also feel the force of **gravity**, which is how they know which way is up. Plant biologists call this **geotropism**.

Most plants can also smell or taste **water** in soil – moving their growing roots towards pockets of water underground. This is called **hydrotropism**. And many also move their roots towards nutrients, and away from harmful chemicals they can smell or taste in the air and soil – something called **chemotropism**.

Perhaps most impressively, many plants also move in response to **touch.**

Most do not move quite as quickly as the Venus flytrap. But they can use their sense of touch to **twist** around obstacles, to **climb** plants and rocks, and to **weave** their roots, **over, under and around** each other beneath the ground. We call this touch-navigation in plants **thigmotropism**. This is how **tomato plants** and **grapevines** climb trellises in the garden, and how **ivy** leaves climb walls, and encircle trees and doorways.

The famous biologist **Charles Darwin** was one of the first scientists to investigate these plant movements (or **tropisms**) back in 1881. But it took scientists more than a century to figure out exactly how plants were doing it. And we are still working it out now.

One of the more recent discoveries is that plants not only **sense** and **move through** their environment, they also **fight**, **cooperate**, and **talk to each other** through massive underground root networks.

Okay, now you're just being silly. Plants can't talk. They don't even make noises!

They do not talk out loud, perhaps, as animals do. But just as humans communicate through the internet with **silent text messages** and **emails**, plants can communicate through a massive network of roots beneath the ground. The roots of individual plants are tied together by **symbiotic fungi**[*]. These helpful little organisms both feed off the tree and help the plant to survive. In this case, they carry **chemical messages** between different plant bodies – even plants of different species.

The thread-like fungi that connect plant roots together are called **mycorrhizae**, and the network is called a **mycorrhizal network**. Some of these networks can be **thousands of metres** or **several miles** across – spanning entire forests underground.

....

* Symbiotic organisms (or symbionts) are the opposite of parasites. Both parasites and symbionts have trouble surviving on their own, so attach themselves to other 'host' organisms to survive. But while parasites harm their hosts, symbionts do not. Rather, they become like helpful friends or housemates – providing a service in exchange for their daily bed and breakfast!

So, errr . . . what do plants talk about?

All sorts of things! They **haggle** for nutrients, **team up** against invading plants, **warn** each other about the spread of diseases, even **ask each other for help**, and **come to the rescue** when needed. Some scientists have discovered that when a young forest tree is **not connected** to this underground 'internet', it **fails to grow and thrive** like the trees around it. And when an **old tree** knows it is dying, it can **donate nutrients** to other nearby trees via this root network. Like a stately old lord, leaving a lifetime of accumulated wealth to its family and friends.

Some of these **mycorrhizal tree networks** are so complex and interconnected that scientists actually think of them as a single **super-organism**. If so, this would make them the largest and oldest organisms on the planet.

A **blue whale**, after all, is only **33 m (100 feet)** long, and weighs a mere **200 tons**, and lives **80 to 90 years**. But one networked colony of **aspen** trees in Utah, USA, covers nearly **430,000 square metres (5 million square feet)**, weighs over **6,000 tons**, and may be over **10,000** years old.

Too cool! Okay, if that's one organism, then we should definitely rename it the Giant Yoda Tree.

Actually, that's not bad. I'll call up my botanist mates and suggest it.

STRANGE AND CRAZY PLANTS OF THE WORLD

Immortal Plant (*Welwitschia mirabilis*)

This Namibian desert plant has two shaggy leaves, and grows in clusters that reach 2 m (6 feet) tall, 8 m (26 feet) across. Oh, and it can live anywhere from 400 to 1,500 years!

Sensitive Plant (*Mimosa pudica*)

The odd plant species, native to Central and South America, has leaves that fold inwards instantly when you touch them, then unfold again minutes later.

Resurrection Plant (*Selaginella lepidophylla*)

A desert plant native to Mexico's Chihuahuan Desert, it curls into a tight ball during dry weather, allowing it to survive months or years of total desiccation (drying out).

Baseball Plant (*Euphorbia obesa*)

This toxic plant is shaped like a small, green ball with eight ridges that look like stitching. Measuring 6–15 cm (2–6 inches) across, it is highly prized by collectors. But since it grows slowly, it has become endangered in its native South Africa.

Corpse Flower (*Amorphophallus titanum*)

Taller than an adult human, this Indonesian plant gives off the smell of rotting flesh to attract carrion flies and beetles. The bugs then pollinate the plant, carrying its seeds to other, stinky corpse-flowers.

WHERE DOES ALL THE SAND IN THE DESERT COME FROM?

Sand is basically powdered rock or soil scraped and blasted from the land by powerful wind. Sandy deserts form over many years of dry weather and wind erosion, piling sand particles into thick sheets and dunes. Not all deserts are hot and sandy places, and not all deserts are formed the same way.

Not all deserts are sandy?

Nope. Some are, certainly. But others are covered with rock pebbles, salt, or even ice.

But if a desert isn't a hot, sandy place then what *is* it?

The word desert describes any dry place where more water **evaporates** than **falls** as rain. Regardless of whether it is **hot** or **cold**, **sandy** or **rocky**, if it gets less than **25 cm (10 inches)** of rain per year, then it is technically a desert.

How many deserts are there?

There is at least one desert on every continent. Most have several. Altogether, deserts cover about one fifth of the land surface on Earth. Depending on where they are in the world, deserts may have different **appearances** and **weather systems**. Some, like China's **Taklamakan Desert** are largely empty. Others, like the **Chihuahuan Desert** in New Mexico, is teeming with desert plants and animals.

But one thing they all have in common is their extreme **dryness**. The **air** in the desert contains almost **no water vapour**, which keeps the humidity close to zero, all year round.

In this environment, you can feel the water leaving your skin, eyes, nose and mouth – leaving your throat parched, your lips cracked, and your skin tight and itchy. With no water vapour in the air, clouds rarely form over deserts. Without the **shade** that clouds provide, daytime temperatures can rise well above **37ºC (100 degrees Fahrenheit)**. And with no clouds to **trap heat** close to the land, even the hottest deserts can drop to anywhere from **0 to -17ºC** at night.

So how do deserts get so sandy?

Dry climates lead to strong, fast-moving winds which rip across the landscape, scouring rock and earth as they go. With few trees or obstacles to block the way, and few plants to hold the soil together, particles of **soil** and **rock** are lifted into the air and scattered across the land in vast **sandstorms** and **dust storms.** As the sand settles, it forms thick sheets and rolling hills (or **dunes**) on the landscape.

These sheets and dunes are constantly shifted and shaped by the winds – edging into nearby fields and grasslands, spreading and expanding the desert over time. The edges of Africa's famous **Sahara Desert**, for example, have shifted southward by around **100 km (62 miles)** since 1950.

Have the deserts always been there?

Actually no. Deserts can come and go.

25,000 years ago, the Sahara Desert was a lush, green landscape filled with **lakes**, **rivers**, and huge, thirsty **oak trees**. There were tons more **elephants**, **lions** and **giraffes** living there (along with a number of species now extinct). But as the world's climate slowly warmed, this 'Green Sahara' got gradually hotter and drier, leaving behind the vast, sandy landscape we see today.

Is that how all deserts are formed, then? By climate change?

Climate change can certainly speed things up. But there are many **different types of desert** in the world, and they can form in very different ways.

Inland (or **interior**) **deserts** form in the middle of a huge landmass or continent, where clouds literally have trouble getting to them. Clouds, as you know, carry water from sea to land in a constant cycle, bursting over high plains and mountains to form rivers that run back to the ocean. But some locations, like China's **Gobi Desert**, are so far from any ocean that clouds just never make it there. They dump their entire, watery bodies over land en route, leaving the centre of the continent parched and dry.

Rain shadow deserts form where mountain ranges block clouds from reaching nearby lands. **Death Valley**, the scorching North American desert that spans parts of California and Nevada, was formed in this way. As warm, wet clouds make their way from the Pacific Ocean towards Death Valley, they have to travel over the tall **Sierra Nevada** mountains.

As they drift up the westward side of this mountain range, the clouds dump almost all of their their water as rainfall. So by the time that warm, wet air from the Pacific passes down the other side, there is practically no water vapour left in it. Because of this, it can be months – or even years – before a single raincloud drifts over Death Valley.

What about the Sahara? How did that get there?

Africa's **Sahara** and **Kalahari** are both **subtropical deserts**, formed by patterns of **heating** and **cooling** near the equator. Close to the equator, plenty of water evaporates into clouds and falls back to Earth as rain. This helps feed the lush **equatorial rainforests** of Africa and South America. But it also causes problems in the areas just north and south of them.

After dumping so much water at the equator, the cold, dry air moving over the Sahara and Kalahari regions **stops clouds from forming** there – leaving the land parched, dry, and exposed to searing temperatures and winds. Climate change has been gradually accelerating this effect for thousands of years. But in the last 150 years, it has sped up dramatically, creating terrible **droughts** in these regions.

The last two types of desert are **coastal** and **polar deserts**.

Coastal deserts form where cold ocean currents chill the air near the shore, resulting in damp, misty fogs that roll in from the sea, but little in the way of actual rainfall. The vast **Atacama Desert** in Chile was formed this way, as was the **Namib Desert** in Africa.

The Atacama Desert gets less than **one millimetre** of rain per year, and it has been known not to rain at all there for **20 years**!

Polar deserts, as the name suggests, are formed at the north and south poles of our planet. There is plenty of fresh water at the poles, but the freezing air locks it into vast **ice sheets**, making it **inaccessible** to plants and animals. The **Arctic** and **Antarctic** are actually the **largest deserts in the world**, with each measuring over **14.2 million square km (5.5 million square miles)** across. The **Arctic** gets just **15–25 cm (6–10 inches)** of rain per year, while the **Antarctic** gets **less than one centimetre** of rain per year – making it drier even than the Sahara, or Death Valley.

So will global warming turn everything into desert in the future?

Not everything, perhaps. But human activities and climate change are creating more and more desert – a process called **desertification**.

Every year, around **6 million square km (2 million square miles)** of land turns to desert due to **overgrazing** grassland with animals, or **overworking** fields and soils.

Grazing removes grass that holds the soil together, while constant tilling and turning the soil for large-scale farming breaks it up, and makes it easier for the winter to erode it. **Deforestation** by loggers and farmers is also a problem, as forest trees and plants help hold the soil together too.

Human overpopulation is another problem. Especially in water-scarce regions, where human towns and cities drain too much groundwater from critical wetlands and plains, creating new **coastal** and **inland deserts**. There are attempts to combat this by **planting trees** to prevent soil erosion and building **fences** to contain the shifting, spreading desert sands.

Hopefully, we will figure it out before we are all living like Luke Skywalker or Rey in Star Wars, scavenging for water and machine parts under the scorching suns of Tatooine.

Well, at least we only have one sun. And there are no Jawas or Sand People here.

Not yet, at least.

What?!?!

Nothing! Never mind . . .

DESERT LIFE

We tend to think of deserts as dry, dead places where nothing lives. But actually, many deserts are teeming with hidden life. Here are just a few things you might find in each type of desert.

Hot and Dry Desert

- Examples: Chihuahuan, Sonoran (USA), Southern Asian, Ethiopian, Australian.
- Plants: yucca, turpentine, prickly pear, agave.
- Animals: mostly burrowers – kangaroo rat, fennec fox, thorny devil lizard.

Semi-Arid Desert

- Examples: Sagebrush, Great Basin (USA), Nearctic (Greenland, Russia).

- Plants: creosote, white thorn, cat claw, mesquite, jujube.
- Animals: burrowers and shade-seekers – rabbit, skunk, sidewinder, burrowing owl.

Coastal Desert

- Examples: Atacama (South America), Namib (Africa).
- Plants: salt bush, rice grass, horsebrush, black sage.
- Animals: reptiles, amphibians, and their predators – coyote, badger, bald eagle, horned owl.

Cold Desert

- Examples: Antarctic, Taklamakan (China).
- Plants: bunchgrass, acacia, pistachio tree, giant carton cactus.
- Animals: more burrowers – jack rabbit, kit fox, pocket mouse, ground squirrel.

WHY CAN'T WE FIX GLOBAL WARMING?

Global warming is a complex problem caused by excess heat trapped in the Earth's atmosphere. Fixing it quickly would mean altering the atmosphere of the entire planet, which is not an easy thing to do. It is possible that we may one day reverse global warming through new and undiscovered technologies. For now, the best we can hope to do is slow it down or stop making it worse.

I don't get it. If it's us that made global warming happen, then why can't we just reverse it, change it back?

That's a fair question to ask, and unfortunately the answer is not a happy one.

Here is what we know: global warming (or **climate change**) is the name we give to a steady rise in global temperatures over time, caused by an increase in so-called **greenhouse gases** (chiefly **carbon dioxide**) in our atmosphere. The Earth's atmosphere traps heat naturally, keeping our planet much warmer than it would otherwise be – something scientists call **the greenhouse effect**. Greenhouse gases, including carbon dioxide, are a big part of what makes that happen. Without them, the Earth would be a giant snowball or a lifeless dry landscape like Mars. So we need the **greenhouse effect** – we just need it not to work quite as well as it has been of late.

Since we started burning coal, oil and gas – right?

Right. Ever since the **Industrial Revolution** about 150 years ago, we have been extracting and burning more and more **fossil fuels** (coal, gas, and oil) and releasing more and more carbon dioxide into the atmosphere. For a while, this did not seem to be a problem.

But over the last **80 years,** our fuel-burning and carbon-spewing has **skyrocketed.** Largely due to millions more people buying cars, flying in aeroplanes, and heating and powering their homes with electricity, worldwide.

Has the atmosphere really changed that much?

Yes, it has. Look at it this way: for most of recorded history, from **ancient Egypt** to the age of **motor cars** and **aeroplanes**, carbon dioxide levels in the atmosphere sat at around **280 parts per million (ppm)**. By **1950**, that had risen to **310 ppm** – a 10% increase, in a little over 100 years. By the 1980s, it had risen to **340 ppm.** Today, it sits at over **410 parts per million** – which is higher than at any point in the last **800,000 years**.

So is that why the world keeps getting hotter?

For the most part, yes. All that extra carbon dioxide that has been blanketing the Earth and steadily driving global temperatures upwards since 1880, has made the last 10 years the **hottest decade in history**. Unfortunately, we cannot **stop** or **reverse** this runaway temperature rise by magically **altering the entire mix of gases** in the atmosphere.

It took us 150 years to make it the way it is. So it will take at least that to get it back to the way it was. Probably 10 times that.

What if we stopped using fossil fuels altogether?

Well, even if we stopped all burning and production of fossil fuels **tomorrow**, experts reckon it would take roughly **1,000 years** for the atmosphere to return to the way it was before 1800.

1,000 years. We can't wait that long! We'll all be frazzled by then!

Right. And that's *if* we stop using fossil fuels completely, right away. In reality, we are simply not going to do that.

Most of the world still relies on fossil fuels to power our mobile, energy-hungry lives. Few of us would be willing to give up the convenience of driving cars, flying in aeroplanes, heating and powering our houses, and having our food delivered to local supermarkets – all using the energy that fossil fuels provide. So stopping fossil fuel use **immediately** is simply not an option for most of the world, and we need another plan. Otherwise, it won't just be a **thousand** years before things go back to normal. It will be **never**.

That's awful! Can we at least stop making it worse?

That, we can do. And we need not necessarily give up everything we enjoy in order to do it. We don't have to give up all **electrical heating** and **power** – we just have to make sure we are not **wasting** energy, and then look for ways of **producing** it that do not involve fossil fuels. This means switching more and more to **clean**, **renewable** sources of energy, and building more **wind turbines**, **solar farms**, and **solar rooftops** to that end.

We don't have to give up all forms of **transport,** either. Not if we design our cities for easier walking and cycling, then provide public **buses**, **trams** and **shuttles** running on **renewable electricity** or **hydrogen fuel**.

We don't have to go back 200 years and farm all our own food. We just have to make an effort to buy it from **local shops and farmer's markets**, rather than supermarkets that ship foods from farms halfway across the world. That way, we hugely reduce the amount of energy used (and carbon released) in getting the food to us.

Making these changes will not stop climate change, of course. But if we do all this now, we may be able to **buy time** to develop **new technologies** that can halt – or even **reverse** – the effects of global warming.

What kinds of technologies?

One idea is to **capture and recycle** most of the **carbon dioxide** we are producing. Right now, factories and power plants just dump carbon dioxide into the atmosphere. You see it in that smoke you see billowing from their massive chimneys and cooling towers.

But if we **capped** those chimneys with special filters, then we could **capture** most of that carbon dioxide, **store** it deep below ground in porous rocks, or **use** it to grow greenhouse plants.

Factories in the UK, US and China are already experimenting with this kind of **carbon capture** technology. Although the process is still in the works, it could eventually cut carbon emissions by up to **70%**, giving time for our forests and oceans to **absorb** and **rebalance** carbon dioxide levels in the atmosphere.

Would that make the planet cool down a bit?

Eventually, yes. But it would might take a century or more for nature to mop up the mess that we have created up there.

In the meantime, another group of scientists and engineers have suggested **reflecting sunlight away** from the Earth, to provide some immediate relief. We could do this by **seeding clouds** over the ocean, creating a natural layer of shade that would reduce sea temperatures, and perhaps slow down polar melting and sea-level rise.

Or we might do it by launching thousands of giant, mirror-like **reflectors** into space, mounted on orbiting **satellites** that keep them between us and the sun at all times.

These **space mirrors** would do nothing to heal our atmosphere. But they might provide relief for farmers with **ruined crops** or countries suffering with seasonal **heatwaves** and **droughts**.

Space mirrors? Crazy. Wouldn't they give us all spotty sunburns, though?

Not likely. The mirrors would be so far away that they would shade entire **cities**, rather than select **body parts**.

The real challenge would be building **enough** of them and getting them all **up** there. Mirrors do not exactly travel well, and rockets are not exactly the smoothest form of transport.

Yeah, imagine if you broke a rocket full of mirrors on the way up there. You'd have, like, 1,000 years of bad luck!

WHOOSH!

Well, if we don't do something about climate change, we could be facing that anyway . . .

CLIMATE CHANGE: THE HARD FACTS

There is still a lot of argument (at least among non-scientists and non-experts) about whether climate change is real, and what is causing it. Here is what 99% of the world's scientists agree on:

What we are seeing:

- The Earth's atmosphere is getting hotter and hotter.
- The Earth's oceans are getting warmer, and more acidic.

What is causing this:

- Carbon dioxide emissions are by far the largest cause of climate change.
- Since 1950, virtually all of the warming we have seen has been caused by human activities.

- Natural forces (changes in solar radiation, volcanic eruptions) have caused virtually none of the temperature rise.
- The largest human sources of carbon dioxide emissions are the direct burning of fossil fuels, making cement, and burning off gases during oil, gas, and petrol production.

How this is impacting the planet:

- Sea levels are rising at an increasing pace.
- Glaciers and polar ice sheets are melting and disappearing.
- The number of cold days and nights is decreasing.
- The number of hot days and nights is increasing.
- Heatwaves are lasting longer.
- Rainstorms and snowstorms are becoming more intense.
- Dry areas are getting drier, wet areas are getting wetter.
- Plant and animal species are vanishing at an ever-increasing rate, unable to adapt quickly enough to cope with the changes.
- Human diseases and health problems are getting worse, with poorer regions and people suffering more than richer ones.

COULD WE EVER MAKE OUR OWN WEATHER?

Weather control is theoretically possible, and some countries are already doing it (or at least trying to do it). You can create rain or keep the skies clear by 'seeding' clouds with chemicals from aeroplanes or rockets. Right now, this weather-control technology is pretty unreliable. One day, we really might have the power of weather-on-demand. The question is: should we use it?

We can really do it? Like, really make our own weather?

Well, not so much make our weather as alter it. But yes – we can change local weather to a point.

What kind of weather? Can we make it sunny when it's raining outside?

No, we can't really do that. But we can make it rain or snow a little, if needed.

Why would you want to *make* it rain?

Actually, lots of reasons. If you live in England, Scotland or Ireland, you probably get plenty of rain, and you generally wish for more sunny days. But in parts of southern Europe, Africa, Asia and the Americas, it sometimes does not rain for **months** or **years** on end.

This creates terrible, crop-withering **droughts**, dangerous **heatwaves**, and massive **wildfires** that destroy homes and animal habitats alike. If you live in one of those places, a little rainfall can be a lifesaver.

For this and other reasons, China, the USA, and other countries have been experimenting with the science of **weather modification** for decades. China even has a massive **Ministry of Weather Modification***, for the sole purpose of **making and diverting rain**.

That's just nuts! So how do they do it?

---

* Which sounds like something from one of the Harry Potter books, but is absolutely real.

Mainly through a process called **cloud seeding**. This involves **spraying or firing chemicals into clouds** to encourage the **crystallization** of ice particles within the cloud. When these particles get big and heavy enough, they then fall out of the cloud as rain or snow.

This is actually how raindrops and snowflakes are formed naturally – crystallizing around tiny particles of dust within the cloud, and then falling to the ground as they get heavier. Artificial **cloud seeding** just speeds things up a bit, making clouds drop water when (and where) they otherwise might not.

Depending on how and when you seed the clouds, you can either **make it rain on demand**, or **break up gathering storm clouds to prevent rainfall** – increasing your chances of having a sunny day.

How do they get the chemicals into the clouds?

Usually in one of two ways. The first is to fly a **crop-spraying aeroplane** over the cloud, dropping the cloud-seeding chemicals from **above**.

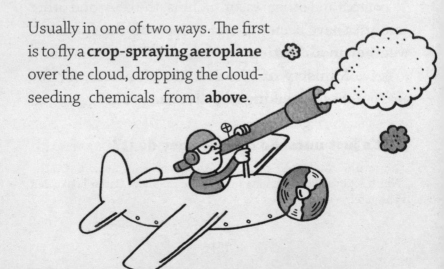

The second is to launch **bazooka shells** or **ground-to-air rockets** at the clouds from **below** – releasing the chemical in one huge explosion.

Well, that sounds like a lot of fun if nothing else! Does it really work?

It can work, but it is hard to tell whether it did work, and how well.

The Chinese Ministry of Weather Modification claims to have created billions of tons of rainfall this way. When the forecast of rain threatened the opening ceremony of the **2008 Summer Olympics** in Beijing, the MWM blasted and seeded clouds for several days ahead of the event. It genuinely seemed to work, as no rain fell on the day of the ceremony.

But who knows whether the rain clouds would have cleared up anyway, even without the Ministry's attempt to disperse them.

Most studies of cloud seeding and weather-modification methods suggest that more than half the time it does not work at all. And when it does, it increases the chances of rain or snow by perhaps 10% at best. Which does not seem like a great result, given the downsides of trying to alter the weather this way.

Like what?

For starters, it's very **expensive**. The main chemical used for seeding clouds is **silver iodide**, a liquid solution of **silver** and **iodine**. You need several **plane-loads** of the stuff to seed a massive cloud system, and plane-loads of silver iodide are not cheap.

Of course, you can save on aeroplane expenses by launching the chemicals into the clouds, inside those ground-to-air rockets. But this has the dangerous side effect of unexploded bombs and missiles falling into your neighbour's farm, or back garden[*].

I can't imagine my parents would be too happy with that. So, will we get better at this? In the future, maybe?

Possibly, yes. Engineers are certainly working on it. Some are researching the use of **microwave lasers** to break up newly forming **tornadoes** – perhaps fired from weather-sensing **satellites** in orbit.

Others have suggested fleets of **robot drone ships,** which can be launched into the path of a growing **hurricane** to spread **biodegradable oils** on the ocean

....

[*] This has actually happened in China. Several times.

PEW
PEW

surface. This, in theory, would decrease **evaporation** from the warm ocean, which feeds a growing hurricane from below. Who knows where it might go. A bigger question to ask is: even if we could control the weather, should we actually do it?

What do you mean?

Okay, let's say you you had the power to control the weather in your hometown. What would you do with that power?

I dunno. I would probably make it sunny all the time. So me and my friends could play outside more. Then also make it snow a bunch of times in the winter. So we could get a load of days off school. Go sledging, have snowball fights . . .

Okay, fine. But what if, by **stopping** the **rain** in your area, you **created** a **thunderstorm** or **flash flood** elsewhere? What if, by **making it snow** six feet in your town, you **stopped any snow or rainfall** from reaching the next town over? Many mountain towns depend on meltwater from snowfall through the winter. Without it, their rivers and wells would run dry in the summer.

Everything on our living planet, including our weather and climate, is unavoidably **linked to everything else**, in **massive**, **complex systems** we do not yet fully understand.

In trying to make the weather better for ourselves, we might accidentally harm **plants**, **animals** and **human populations** that depend on their local climate **staying just the way that it is**.

Given that we are already messing with our climate and weather patterns through the unhappy accident of **global warming**, many scientists say we should be careful about messing with it further. At least for now.

Okayyyy. I guess I would probably leave the weather the way it is, then ...

... just maybe a pause button, or little fast-forward for the rain, once in a while?

WEATHER CONTROL

Weather modification is a tricky business. Here is a quick guide to what we can (and cannot) do with today's technology.

WE CAN:

Make it rain (a bit)

Cloud seeding can encourage rain in certain climates and conditions. But it doesn't work all the time, and we can't control how much cloud cover is produced.

Trigger lightning strikes

We can make lightning on demand by firing rockets (with metal wires on them) into growing thunderclouds. But this only helps us study lightning. It cannot be used to prevent lightning strikes, or to make them zap something specific.

Create clouds

Water vapour collecting over power stations can lead to the formation of 'artificial' cloud layers called fumulus clouds. As these get blown over land, they can condense and may rain or snow in areas close to the power station. Not often a helpful effect, but it happens.

WE CANNOT:

Create flash floods

Even with massive cloud-seeding and rain-making efforts, we cannot generate anywhere near enough cloud formation to trigger a flash flood.

Create hurricanes

Hurricanes are massive super-storms, hundreds of miles across. They are created by massive evaporation from tropical oceans, not by evil governments or supervillains.

Trigger tsunamis (tidal waves)

Tsunamis are created by earthquakes – massive releases of energy caused by shifts in the Earth's crust. We cannot make earthquakes happen, so we cannot make tsunamis happen either.

Stop tornadoes

Though we have got much better at predicting where tornadoes might form and touch down, we have no way of stopping their formation, or their rampage across the landscape. One scientist suggested building a massive wall across the middle of America (where the most tornadoes form) to stop tornadoes there. But aside from being insanely expensive, that probably wouldn't help much, since tornadoes often 'jump' over ground-based obstacles.

WHAT'S THE THE BIGGEST NUMBER OF PEOPLE WE COULD FIT ON EARTH?

The Earth isn't getting any bigger. But its human population is. If we keep going the way we are, we could reach 10 billion or more people by the year 2100. Whether the planet can cope with that many people remains to be seen, as it has never carried that many before. It all depends on how we choose to live, work, eat, produce and use our energy.

I don't get it. Why are there so many people on the planet now? Where are they all coming from?

Put simply, we are multiplying faster than we're dying off. For most of human history, which started around

300,000 years ago, the number of humans on the planet has been kept in check by **famine** (or **starvation**), **diseases**, **old age**, and **dangerous rival tribes and species**. In other words, the same limits and dangers faced by most other animals on the planet. Humans have always multiplied. But until a few hundred years ago, these limits and dangers kept the human population at fewer than a billion people worldwide. But now the brakes are off, and human populations are **exploding**.

So what changed?

It started with the development of **farming** and **agriculture**, about 10,000 years ago. Around that time, we got a lot better at growing and **harvesting** our food, rather than having to **hunt** and **scavenge** for it. This allowed us to stay put, and to build bigger villages and towns. We went from roaming around in **bands** of **6 to 12 people**, to living in **civilizations** of **10,000** people or more.

With civilization came **technology** and **medicine**. With these, we started doing even better. Cities of thousands became **nations** of millions, tens of millions, even **hundreds of millions**.

Granted, we still had regular famines and wars. And not everyone, everywhere, thrived in the same numbers.

But still, the total number of humans on the planet continued to grow, and we carved out new homelands in even the furthest reaches of the planet.

The development of machine-powered factories and farms allowed us to produce even more food, and get it to even more people over ever-longer distances. While the development of **vaccines** and **antibiotics** allowed us to **treat** – and even **wipe out** – diseases that had plagued humans for centuries.

Between 1800 and 1900, the global population **doubled**. In the century since then, it has **quadrupled**. By the year 2100, there could be **10 billion** or more human beings walking the planet.

Okay, that seems like a lot. Can the planet handle that many people?

The Earth will be just fine. The planet is not going to collapse under the weight of us. But the **living systems** we depend upon to feed and support those billions of humans just might collapse. Systems like the **soil** that grows our food, the **oceans** that provide our fish, and the **forests** that provide our oxygen. If these critical systems were to collapse, the planet would eventually recover. But human civilization might not.

So how many people *can* the planet handle?

Honestly? Nobody knows. We have never run this experiment before, and there are already **billions** more humans on the planet than there have ever been.

Some say the planet could support **11 billion** people before **overfishing**, **overfarming**, and **water availability** became a problem. Others say the planet could handle **13 billion** or more. It all depends **how** those people live, and how much **food**, **energy**, and **water** they use.

Why's that?

Well, right now many of the fastest growing regions in the world are in developing countries. By 2050, there will be an additional **1.9 billion** people on the planet, almost all of these extra people in developing regions of **Africa** (1.2 billion), and **Asia** (0.7 billion).

If that explosion of people was happening in North America or Australia instead, then we would be in **serious** trouble. This is because the average person in the USA or Australia uses **4–5 times** as much **energy** and **8–10 times** as much **water** as the average person living in Africa or Asia. If everybody on Earth lived the way most Americans, Australians, and Europeans do, then the planet could support maybe **two or three billion people** at the most.

As it is, there are only **1.4 million** Americans, Australians and Europeans living these high-energy lives. The other **6.4 billion** are, thankfully, consuming a lot less. But that is changing fast – especially in parts of India, China, and Indonesia. Put simply, most scientists agree that we have **already stretched the capacity** of the planet to support us, and we really do not know **where the breaking point is**.

So what can we do? Stop people from having babies?

We could try. But then who decides which families get to have babies, and which ones do not? Past attempts at controlling populations this way have shown that however you try to do it, it is very hard to make that decision fair for everyone, and the effort will backfire in the end. More likely, populations will just **keep growing** for as long as we have the capacity to support them.

So then how do we make room for 10 billion people?

That is the critical question. We can start by making our homes, vehicles, and lives **more efficient** and **less**

wasteful. That way, there will be **more energy** and **water** to go around and **less waste** created per person.

Shifting to **renewable energy sources** like solar power and wind power will be especially important, as without this step, our **fuel supplies** will soon run out, and the **pollution** caused by 10 billion people will be immense.

We may also have to get clever about how we **feed** and **house ourselves** – engineering new types of **food crops** that need less **water** and **space** to grow. We will need more compact, efficient living spaces. Perhaps buildings that stretch far above (or tunnel far below) the ground, rather than sprawling out across the surface. Maybe we will combine the two – **growing food** on the **walls** and **roofs** of our apartments, and **recycling water** from our gutters, drains and bathrooms. It could all get very space-age before the century is out.

Hmmm. Couldn't we just move a bunch of people to Mars, or some other planet?

Maybe. But then we would be facing all the same problems somewhere else. Somewhere with an even harsher climate, a hostile atmosphere, and little water or food beyond what we took with us to grow. And let's face it – the Earth is, at least for now, a much prettier place to live.

ACTIVITY:
WATCHING THE WORLD EXPLODE

If you want to see the increase in world population each second, you can visit the US Census Bureau's World Population Clock at:

https://www.census.gov/popclock/

How much does the world population increase in one minute?

World Population

3,532,081

How many people is that in one second? In one day? In one week?

Now look at the graph of Historical Estimates of World Population at:

http://www.ciese.org/curriculum/popgrowthproj/worldpop/

In which years did the world's population suddenly start to increase?

What might have been the reasons for these explosions?

QUICK ONES –
PLANTS, HABITATS, AND CLIMATE

How do cactuses live in the desert with no water?

Cactuses, like all living things on Earth, need water to survive. But thanks to some very nifty adaptations, they are able to survive in deserts and arid regions that receive little or no rainfall each year. Below the ground, their roots fan out 5 m (15 feet) or more, drawing as much water as possible from parched, sandy soils. Above the ground, they have thin, prickly spines instead of leaves. Since plants lose most of their water by evaporation from their leaves' surfaces, the spines help reduce water loss during the scorching desert days. And when it eventually does rain in the desert, cactuses can store huge amounts of water inside their succulent, hollow bodies. A single saguaro cactus can store up to 750 litres (500 gallons) of water! Good to know if you ever find yourself lost in the desert with no Evian . . .

Why do dead trees rot and go mouldy?

Dead trees rot for much the same reason as dead animals do – because their bodies are invaded and overgrown by decomposers (bacteria and fungi) that feed on dead things. While the tree is alive, it repels these tiny colonizers by making special chemicals – natural antibiotics and fungicides – that stop bacterial and fungal cells from growing. But when the tree dies, it stops making these protective chemicals, and the lodgers move in to feed. The layers of hairy mould you see on dead trees is actually a type of living fungus (or several species of fungus) feeding on the plant sugars and proteins trapped in the dead tree's body. And where bacteria and fungi eat away at the tree, dark patches, brittle fibres, and gaping holes remain – which we recognize as rot. The same thing happens to human and animal bodies after we die, too. It's just that we bury them to keep them out of sight, and to prevent the spread of disease. But no one puts dead trees in coffins. (That would be weird, since coffins are made of dead trees anyway.)

Why don't trees grow on mountain tops?

Trees are not fond of high winds, low temperatures, or dry air – all of which you find in mountain-top environments. Generally speaking, the taller the tree, the more water it needs, the less tolerant it is of cold weather, and the easier it breaks in high winds. As you trek further and further up a mountainside and feel the air getting colder and drier, you can actually see the trees getting smaller and stumpier. Eventually, you reach a point (called the **timberline**), above which no trees can grow. Upwards from that point, all you see is rocks and low-lying scrub plants. Some trees – like poplars, aspens, and birches – have evolved to survive at higher, drier altitudes than most. But even they disappear above a certain height, and you won't see any of them growing atop Mount Hood, Mount Fuji, or Mount Everest.

Before humans came along, was the whole world just forest?

Forests still cover about one third of the Earth's surface. But 300,000 years ago – before modern humans evolved – close to two thirds of the planet was forested. There is little doubt that humans – slashing and burning to create new farmland, and logging entire forests for wood, paper, and fuel – are responsible for most of that tree loss. But 3 million years ago, long before humans arrived, thick forests covered the grasslands (savannahs) of Africa and Asia, and the great plains of North America. The forests started to dwindle when the climate began to cool off. But human activities have accelerated that dwindling, especially since the age of steam and industry began, around 250 years ago. Which is one reason why we need to protect our remaining forests, and even replant them to get things back to the way they were.

How much hotter will the world be in 100 years?

That all depends on what we do in the next 25–50 years. Things are definitely heating up, driven by a growing global population, our increasing appetite for food, power, and transport, and our ongoing use of fossil fuels to supply them. All of this is driving up levels of greenhouse gases (especially carbon dioxide), increasing the greenhouse effect and heating up our atmosphere and oceans. Even if we drastically reduce our power production (or shift to cleaner, greener, renewable power sources like wind and solar power), then the world will still be around 3–4 degrees warmer by 2100 than it is now. If we do nothing, and keep using and producing power the way we are now, then it could be as much as 9 degrees hotter by 2100. That might not sound like much, but even a few degrees' temperature change can be enough to melt trillions of tonnes of ice at the poles, raising sea levels by **20 cm (7 inches)** or more. With a 9-degree rise, sea levels could rise **1–1.2 m (3–4 feet)** – enough to flood huge areas of New York, Hong Kong, and Tokyo. In 100 years' time, over 800 million people, in over 570 cities worldwide, could find themselves homeless and sweltering thanks to climate change. So the world had better get its act together!

ENERGY, POWER, AND MACHINES

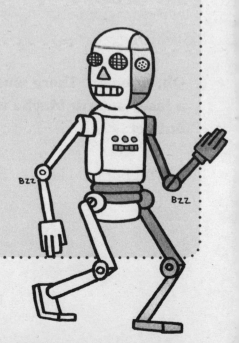

BZZ

BZZ

COULD YOU REALLY MAKE A LIGHTSABER?

Exciting as they are in the movies, lightsabers are not really possible in real life. Lasers cannot form solid shapes, make air glow, or crash into each other the way lightsabers seem to do. We could make plasma swords instead. But just holding one would likely burn your hand off.

Oh, come on. There must be *some* way of making a laser-sword. Maybe we just haven't figured it out yet.

Maybe. But not likely.

Why not?

Well for starters, lasers simply do not look and behave the way lightsaber blades do on-screen, and you will never get them to. **Laser beams** are beams of focused light, and light cannot take on a fixed shape or length. So if lightsaber blades really were laser-swords, then when you switched them on, the blades would look more like **torches** or **laser pointers**. The blade would not stop in mid-air a few feet from your hand. It would extend all the way to the wall or the ceiling. And just like a laser pointer, you would not see a glowing beam of coloured light, carving its way through the air. Just a spot on the wall (or perhaps your enemy's body) where the laser hilt is pointed.

But you can see laser beams sometimes, can't you? I've seen lasers on TV at concerts and stuff.

If the air is filled with smoke, then you can see the path of the laser beam as it bounces off smoke particles in the air. Similarly if you shine one through cloudy water. But in thin air, you would see nothing but the end-point – the place where the beam first hits something. Usually the wall or ceiling.

What exactly is a laser, anyway?

Lasers are unusual, man-made light sources, which emit narrow beams of coloured light. Where a torch emits white light (which is a mixture of all frequencies of visible light), lasers produce beams of a single frequency and colour – such as red or green[*]. To make a laser, you need two things:

- A tube full of **solid crystal or gas atoms**, with a mirror at either end
- An **energy source**, also known as a **pump source** or **flash lamp**

A Nd:YAG solid-state laser

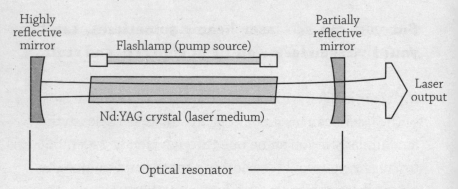

Highly reflective mirror

Flashlamp (pump source)

Partially reflective mirror

Laser output

Nd:YAG crystal (laser medium)

Optical resonator

....

[*] Though you can also make lasers that emit invisible ultraviolet or infrared light, too.

Put simply, the flash lamp excites the atoms in the tube, which release tiny packets of light (called **photons**) as they quickly calm back down again. Once released, these photons whizz back and forth between the mirrors, bashing into even more excitable atoms, and causing them to release even more photons. Physicists call this **stimulated emission**. It happens super fast – creating a kind of chain reaction that concentrates and amplifies the light inside the laser tube, all within milliseconds (thousandths of a second) of switching on the laser. It is this **amplification** that makes laser light different from natural, white light. And this is where lasers get their name – the word '**LASER**' actually stands for **L**ight **A**mplification by **S**timulated **E**mission of **R**adiation.

Cool. But how does the light get out of the tube if there is a mirror at both ends?

Well spotted. One of them is a partial mirror, which reflects some photons of light, while letting some escape. Those escaping photons form the narrow beam of concentrated laser light. A beam you can use to **transmit information**, **scan barcodes**, **read DVDs**, or even **cut through metal and glass**.

Aha! So you *can* cut things with laser beams!

Yes, you can. But not by swinging them through things like a metal sword.

Why not?

Because swords are **massive**, **solid objects**. When a sword crashes into another solid object, the thin, wedge-shaped blade splits the structure of that object, breaking the bonds between molecules of wood, flesh, or bone as it goes. Depending on how hard (and how straight) you swing it, the wedge might get stuck a few centimetres into the object, or cleave right through it.

Lasers are not **solid objects**. They are **focused beams of light**. They have no mass, no weight, and no impact when you swing them at things. When a laser 'cuts', it does so by **heating up the surface** of an object, boring a hole in its structure as the molecules within are burned up (or **vaporized**) by the concentrated beam.

You can use this targeted heating-burning effect in all sorts of different ways. You can etch patterns into a metal or wood surface, as in **laser engraving**. You can shape delicate, microscopic body tissues, as in **laser eye surgery**. And you can create cracks and fractures in sheets of **glass**. But none of these things happen in an instant. You have to **focus** the beam and hold it there for long enough to burn a hole or a crack in something. If you swipe a laser beam across something, it does not split in two. You just see a tiny dot move across it – possibly pursued by an excitable cat.

WHOOSH

Since they are made of light, laser beams cannot bounce or crash into each other, either. So lightsaber duels would be pretty short-lived.

Boo. Okay, fine. Couldn't you make a lightsaber another way? With something besides lasers?

Well, you might be able to use a **plasma** – to make a kind of **plasma sword.** Plasmas are super-heated gases that conduct electricity. **Lightning** is a plasma. But so is the glowing gas inside **fluorescent lighting tubes**.

With small amounts of electricity running through them, plasmas just emit a pleasant glow, and very little heat. But with enough energy supplied to them, plasmas can reach **thousands of degrees** in temperature – hot enough to melt through flesh, bone, or steel. In fact, there are already **plasma torches** and **plasma cutters** that can do just that.

Sweet! So could you just put a plasma in a tube, like a strip light, and make it into a lightsaber that way?

Possibly. But the kind of super-hot plasma that can cut through bones would need a massive power supply, and would be very difficult to contain. You could maybe do it with massive batteries and electromagnets (which might make a magnetic field powerful enough to stop the plasma from expanding into the air around you). But even if that worked, you would have to recharge the battery after about three seconds – which is probably not long enough for an epic battle with Darth Vader. Worse yet, a plasma hot enough to slice through someone else would also radiate heat back at you. It would be like holding a bolt of lightning in your hand. Your hands, face, and eyes would be horribly burned as soon as you switched it on.

But what if you wore heat-proof armour and helmets? Like one of those suits that scientists wear when they go near volcanoes?

Maybe. But now you are starting to look more like a stormtrooper than a Jedi. Perhaps you should just get a regular, metal sword and become a ninja or a Samurai instead. That seems a lot easier . . .

Really? I'm allowed to have a real sword?

No, you're not. I was joking . . .

Booooo.

ALL ABOUT LASERS

● Lasers were not invented by a single person. The idea for them emerged from the work of three scientists, who shared the Nobel Prize for their invention in **1964**. The first laser was actually built in **1960**.

- Lasers are grouped into classes, based on how powerful they are. **Class 1** lasers are safe, and will not damage your eyes if they are accidentally aimed at you. **Class 4** lasers can burn through metal and start fires in seconds.

- The world's most powerful laser is in China, and is called the **Superintense Ultrafast Laser Facility (SULF)**. A single pulse releases 5.3 petawatts of power – equivalent to **100 trillion light bulbs**!

- Engineers and soldiers use lasers to find the **precise range (or distance)** to a far-away object by shooting a laser pulse at it, calculating the time it takes to bounce back, and dividing that number by the speed of light.

- Astronauts from the Apollo missions left an array of mirrors on the moon, so that we could **fire lasers at them from Earth**, and measure our exact distance from the moon at any time. From this, we learned that the moon is slowly edging away from us, year by year.

WHAT HAPPENS WHEN AN AEROPLANE'S ENGINES STOP WORKING?

Most aircrafts have more than one engine, so they can keep flying even if an engine stops. But even after losing all engine power, an aeroplane will not just drop like a stone. Most aircrafts (even helicopters!) can glide a pretty good distance with no engine power at all, giving the pilot time to descend and land.

I don't get it. Don't aeroplanes need engines to get into the sky?

Yes, they do. Engines provide the forward-pushing force (or **thrust**) that aeroplanes need to take off. Without them, the aeroplane would be unable to get going, let alone get into the air.

Then how can they stay in the air without engines?

Think about it – how do paper aeroplanes stay in the air without engines?

Er . . . they glide. You throw them, and they glide back to the ground.

Right. In a way, that is what aeroplanes are – powered gliders. It is not really the engines that create the upward force (or **lift**) that keeps an aeroplane in the air. It is the shape of its wings, and the airflow deflected by the wings that lifts the aeroplane upwards. The engines just provide that initial boost (like a throw), which gets the plane moving through the air, and the air moving around the wings.

But paper aeroplanes don't stay up forever. They come back down pretty quickly.

True. But if you build them well enough – and launch them properly – they don't just drop out of the air the second they lose momentum. Instead, they glide down to the ground in a gradual line or spiral. With a strong enough throw, a paper aeroplane can glide **70 m (225 feet)** or more before touching down.

Yeah, but paper aeroplanes are super light, and you can't put a person in one. That wouldn't work for a real plane, would it?

Actually, yes. The first true aeroplanes, invented by **Orville and Wilbur Wright** over 100 years ago, were basically powered gliders. The Wright brothers built and tested their vehicles as **gliders** first, then added engines to create the famous **Wright Flyers** later.

The bodies and wings of the flyer were built of lightweight wood and cloth. Only the two, small engines were made of metal. The Wright brothers were brave, but they were not crazy. They knew that if an engine failed on their Flyer, they could still glide it gently back to earth without crashing.

Okay, fine. But you can't glide a massive, metal plane with tonnes of passengers in it. Can you?

Yes, you can. And further than you might think! Even a huge, heavy airliner like the Airbus A380 becomes a glider if it loses engine power. Fully loaded with passengers, an A380 weighs over **570,000 kilograms (570 tonnes)**, and cruises at around **35,000 feet (10,600 m)** above the ground. If an A380 were to lose all engine power at that altitude, it could actually glide for another **30 minutes** – or a distance of **177 km (110 miles)** – before coming down to earth. Granted, the landing would be too hard, too fast, and more than a little dangerous. But it wouldn't just drop from the sky like a stone. It would glide – and the pilot could still steer it all the way down.

Also, the chances of your aeroplane losing all engine power is pretty low. This is because most passenger aeroplanes have more than one engine. The Airbus A380 has **four engines**. Some airliners and cargo aeroplanes have **six**. And all of those engines work independently. Which means if one of them fails, the others keep working. In a multi-engine aircraft, the pilot can even shift power to the remaining engines, so that there is hardly any drop in speed. So smoothly that the passengers might not even notice! Only tiny, light aircraft like the **Cessna Skyhawk** have a single engine. True – if your engine failed in one of those, you would be in trouble. But light aircraft tend not to fly so far, and stay closer to the ground than jet airliners.

What if the wings fell off instead?

The wings **can't** fall off an aircraft any more than your arms can fall off your body. The wings are part of the aeroplane's body. The wings of an A380, for example, are built with strong, flexible spars that thread through the tube-like body (or fuselage) of the aircraft.

So while engines and wheels can, in theory, fall off the body of an aircraft, wings cannot. (Thankfully, engines rarely fall off either – they are very strongly fastened to the wings!)

So aeroplanes are actually really safe, then?

On average, yes. Travelling by aeroplane is many, many times safer than travelling by car. Your chances of being in a deadly **air crash** are about **1 in 11 million**. Your chances of being in a deadly **car crash** are about **1 in 100**, and a deadly **bicycle** accident, **1 in 34**. So yes – aeroplanes are very safe, compared with other ways of getting around.

What about helicopters? I mean, they can't glide can they?

Helicopters do not have wings, so it might seem like the engine is the only thing keeping them in the air. But in fact, the spinning rotors attached to the engine act like rotating wings. So if a helicopter engine stops working, the pilot can disengage the engine and let the rotors spin freely. Pushed by the air rushing up from beneath, the rotors start to spin backwards (this is called **autorotation**). Amazingly, this free-wheeling rotor spin can provide enough **lift** to float the helicopter gently down to earth. So while helicopters are not quite as safe as aeroplanes, crashes are still pretty rare, and they are still a surprisingly safe way to travel, compared to cars and bikes!

Okay, but what if the engine *falls* off a helicopter? Or the rotors get stuck . . .

Then it's time to bust out the parachutes, as you are now in a flying rock.

Haha! I knew it!

PHEW

ALL ABOUT FLIGHT

- At any given time, there are over 8,000 planes in the air, across the globe.

- Take-off and landing are the most dangerous parts of each flight. Roughly half of all aeroplane accidents happen on landing, and another 13% happen during take-off. Which is why you should stay buckled up and alert until you get to cruising altitude.

- On most commercial flights, at an altitude of 30,000 feet (9,000 m) you are about 7% of the way into space. Military flights go a bit higher, but not much.

SG-8

● Aeroplane doors cannot be opened during flight – even if you want them to. Not only are they locked between take-off and landing, the pressure difference between the inside of the cabin and the outside of the plane makes it almost impossible.

● The average lifespan of a commercial jet airliner is 51,000 flight hours, or 20 years. Aeroplanes can remain airworthy far beyond that age. But airlines tend to retire them and buy new ones, just in case.

● Only 5% of the world's population have ever been on an aeroplane. So if you are among them, count yourself lucky!

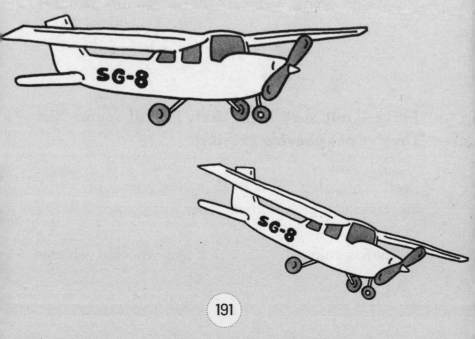

HOW DO MOTORBIKES LEAN OVER WITHOUT FALLING OVER?

Motorbikes can only lean over when they are in motion, and turning into a curve. Lean one over from a standstill, and they topple just like everything else. This gives us some clue as to what is going on. Physicists believe the turning motion of the bike creates a balancing force, which stops the bike from toppling out of a lean. In short, it is pretty weird!

Errrr – not sure I get that. It still seems like they're not obeying gravity!

Yeah, cornering bikes and motorcycles are weird. However you look at them, they just do not seem to make sense!

The first thing to notice is that **two-wheeled vehicles**

(bicycles and motorcycles) are balanced differently from **four-wheeled ones** (cars and trucks). With four wheels, the weight of the car is spread between four points of contact (the lowest point of each tyre). So at a standstill, a car is like a table. It cannot topple over, unless you lift it from beneath. Even when it is in motion, a car keeps most of that four-point stability. Cars might skid, spin, and lose their grip on the road if they brake too fast. But they rarely fall over on their side. Not unless you turn way too fast (more on that in a minute).

Bikes, on the other hand, only have two points of contact with the ground. When you are sitting on a bike at rest, you have to put your feet out to either side (making a total of four contact points) to stop it toppling to one side or the other. Or at the very least, use a **kick-stand** to make three points of contact. This is also why kids start by riding tricycles or bikes with stabilizers (training wheels). Moving tables and tripods stay up without much effort. But balancing on two thin wheels in a line takes effort. You have to use muscles in your arms, legs, and hips to pull the bike upright every time it threatens to topple to one side. In other words, gravity is trying to make the bike fall over, and you have to balance that force with regular pulling forces from your muscles.

So why is it easier to balance on a bike once you get moving?

Once you start rolling (or pedalling), the forward spin of the wheels creates something called a **gyroscopic effect**. The **faster** the wheel spins, the more it **resists turning** and **twisting**. This helps keep the wheels upright, and it means you need less pressure from your arms and legs to keep the bike balanced. If you are going fast enough, you can even take one or both hands off the handlebars, riding **one-handed** or **no-handed** (though this also means you cannot steer or stop the bike, so be careful when you do it!).

Hmmm. Okay – I get that, I think. But that *still* doesn't explain how bikes can lean over and not fall down.

Right – it doesn't. It explains how a bike can stay upright, but not how it can stay balanced at an angle. A motorcycle cornering at top speed can lean over anywhere from 45 degrees (halfway over) to 60 degrees (flat enough for the rider's knee to scrape the ground!). So how can it do that without just dumping onto its side?

Exactly!

It all comes down to the forces pushing and pulling on the bike as it turns. The first and most important force is **gravity**. As you know, gravity pulls everything on Earth towards its centre – which from our point of view is straight down. The second major force acting on the bike is its **acceleration**. This is the force, provided by the engine, carried to the wheels, and delivered to the ground by the tyres.

Now you may remember from our previous book **Isaac Newton's** famous **third law**. If not, it goes like this: **for every action, there is an equal and opposite reaction.** In other words, every force has an equal and opposite force – even if it's hard to see at first.

When the bike is driving **straight**, **gravity** pulls neatly down through the centre of the bike, and **the ground pushes straight back up** through the tyres, wheels, and structure of the bike. The tyres grip the road with **friction**, which pushes the road **backwards**, and accelerates the bike straight **forwards**. Easy-peasy.

But when the bike accelerates into a curve, some new forces come into play. As the rider tries to push the bike **towards the inside of the curve**, another force starts to fling the bike **towards the outside of the curve**. This force is called the **centrifugal force**, and it is the same one that flings you off a spinning merry-go-round, if you don't hold on tight enough.

Now remember when we said cars do not roll or topple over?

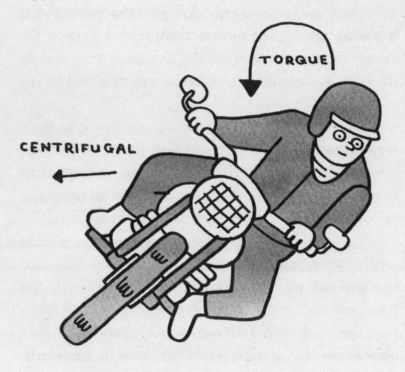

. . . unless you try to turn them way too fast?

Right. You have probably seen this in movies, when the bad guys chasing the good guy try to take a corner too fast, and the car flips up on to two wheels and rolls on to its roof (sometimes two or three times, for dramatic effect). Think for a minute – which way do they always roll when they do that?

They roll away from the corner. Like the wind is blowing them over or something.

Right again. As the car tries to turn hard left, the centrifugal force throws them outwards, to the right. With enough speed and force, this can lift the two wheels closest to the corner off the ground, and flip the car right over.

Compared to stable, four-wheeled cars, wobbly, two-wheeled motorcycles are much easier to tip over this way. As soon as a motorbike turns into a curve, the centrifugal force starts to tip and push the bike towards the outside of it. So if the rider tries to turn while keeping the bike straight (without leaning the bike), then that centrifugal force will tip the bike outwards, and throw the rider off the bike. To prevent this, the rider starts to lean towards the inside of the curve, just as they start to feel that outward-tipping centrifugal force.

If the rider adjusts the lean angle just right, they can create a balance between the forces (gravity, friction) pulling the bike into the curve, and the opposing (centrifugal) force pushing the bike out of the curve. This is how the motorcycle can stay balanced as it accelerates through a curve – even when it is leaning over at a seemingly insane angle. In fact, the faster and harder the rider takes a curve, the more they have to lean into it.

That is pretty crazy. So what happens if the rider forgets to lean over?

The bike misses the curve and crashes.

And what if they lean over too much?

The bike falls flat and crashes.

What if they go too fast?

The bike misses the curve and crashes.

. . . and what if they go too slow?

The bike falls flat and crashes.

Hmmm. Seems like there are a lot of ways to crash on a motorcycle.

Yep. You know how we said aeroplanes were the safest form of travel? Well for this reason and others, motorcycles are right at the other end of the scale. It takes a lot of skill to ride one, and even then you can get unlucky. One icy patch of road, or one misjudged corner, and you crash. And there are no seatbelts or airbags to protect you when you do.

So if you ever decide to get one, take as many safety lessons, and wear as much safety gear as you can. Motorcycles are fast, noisy, and super-fun to watch. But if you want to get around quickly and safely, it is far easier to do it on four wheels than two.

MOTORCYCLE MADNESS

● German inventor Gottlieb Daimler built the first
practical motorcycle in 1885.

- Early motorcycle helmets were lined with cork to absorb impact (now they're lined with high-density foam).

- The longest journey ever made on a motorcycle was by Argentinian adventurer Emilio Scotto, who covered 735,000 km (457,000 miles) across 214 countries, between January 1985 and April 1995.

- Motorcycle stuntman and daredevil Evel Knievel (born Robert Craig Knievel) – famous for ramp-jumping over 10 or 20 cars at a time – still holds the world record for breaking the most number of bones and surviving. In the 15 years between 1965 and 1980, he spent a total of three years in hospital.

- Statistically, motorcyclists are over **30 times** more likely to die in an accident compared to other motorists.

- Japanese engineers once built a motorcycle powered entirely by human excrement. It was called the Toilet Bike Neo, and could travel 300 km before refilling. Which is about when you would need to stop for a poo anyway . . .

WILL WE MAKE ANTI-GRAVITY VEHICLES SOME DAY?

It is impossible to 'cancel out' the force of gravity, which makes 'anti-gravity' cars, bikes, and boots technically impossible. But it is possible to balance the force of gravity with electromagnetic repulsion – something we are already doing with floating trains and hoverboards. You just can't take them off the tracks.

Why can't we cancel out gravity?

In books and movies, floating cars and speeder-bikes stay up using some kind of all-purpose anti-gravity field. In real life, things are not that simple. **Gravity** is an ever-present feature of our world, and of the entire universe. It is one of the four **fundamental forces** of physics, which seems to hold the universe and its contents together.

While we do not yet understand everything about

the force of gravity, we do know largely how it works: **all objects with mass are attracted to each other, with a strength proportional to how massive those objects are**. All sorts of things – including **trees**, **skyscrapers**, **animals**, and **people** – remain stuck to the surface of Earth because the planet itself has mass, and generates a powerful **gravitational field**. Try to push or pull something away from the Earth, and it quickly starts falling back towards the surface, pulled by that gravitational field. Earth-bound **cars**, **trains** and **aeroplanes** are no exception. You can't just switch off the planet's gravity*. It is always there, always pulling. What goes up must come down.

* If you did switch it off, then everything would float off into space!

What you can do is supply another force – one strong enough to **counteract** gravity and push a vehicle away from the planet – at least temporarily.

So how could we do that?

Actually we are already doing it, in at least four different ways. The **first way** to oppose gravity is by heating a gas (or mixture of gases) in a big, upturned sack. As the gas in the bag heats up, it becomes **lighter** and **less dense**. If the gas in the sack becomes lighter than the air in the atmosphere around it, then the sack will begin to rise. This is because the atmosphere, held tight to the Earth's surface, will actually jostle and push the lighter object out of its way – lifting the object away from the Earth's surface and high into the sky. Tie a basket (or a cockpit) to the sack, and you can lift **machinery**, **video cameras**, even **people** into the air along with it. This is how **hot air balloons**, **weather balloons**, and **blimps** work. You can go pretty high in there, too. **Weather balloons** can reach altitudes of **40 km (25 miles)** – which is two thirds of the way into space!

The **second way** to counteract gravity is by creating a flow of air pressure across curving, blade-like wings or rotors. By pushing (or **deflecting**) air downwards, you can create an equal and opposite force called **lift.** As the name suggests, this force can lift a vehicle into the sky and keep it there. **Aeroplanes**, **helicopters** and **drones** all work this way, using chemical **fuels** to create movement in **propeller blades**, which in turn push **air** past **wings** or **rotors** to create lift.

What about rockets, how do they work?

Rockets use a third (and somewhat simpler) way of opposing gravity.

The body of a rocket contains tonnes of **rocket fuel** in the form of liquid or compressed gases. To lift off, the rocket simply detonates that fuel, creating an **explosion** that throws hot gases and air pressure **downwards** and propels the rocket in the **opposite direction**.

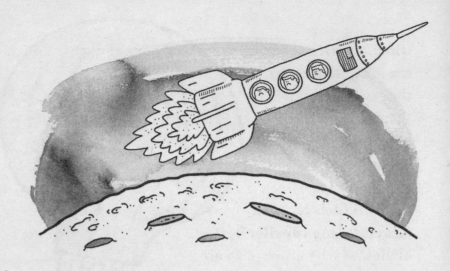

Hold on – wouldn't the rocket just fall back down once all the fuel had exploded? And what stops it from blowing the whole rocket up, into little bits?

Good point! Those were tough questions for early rocket scientists and astronauts to solve, and many of them found out the answers the hard way. Eventually, they figured out that rockets can keep their exploding fuel under control by detonating it a little at a time, in continuous bursts of explosions. This stops the fuel from blowing up the whole rocket, and keeps the rocket accelerating steadily upwards, into space. Or at least until the fuel runs out.

Okay, so that's *three* ways to beat gravity. So what's the fourth?

The **fourth way** is by using magnetic repulsion to create a **magnetic levitation** (or **maglev**) vehicle, which can **hover** above the ground, and float without hot air, aeroplane engines, or rocket fuel.

Whoa! Can we really do that?

Yep, we already have! **Maglev trains** have been around for at least 40 years. There are maglev trains running right now in **China**, **South Korea**, and **Japan**.

They have **switchable electromagnets** attached to the bottom instead of wheels, and they run on special tracks lined with electromagnets that flick from positive to negative, pushing and pulling the floating vehicle along. Since there is almost no friction between the wheels and tracks, like on regular trains, they can go very fast and reach speeds of up to **375 mph (600 km per hour)**.

Awesome! So why can't we just put magnets on cars and make flying cars the same way?

In theory, we can, but it would be very expensive, and the cars could only float, not fly.

Since magnets only repel **other magnets** (or magnetized metals), you would have to line every road with magnets to make this work. That would be very expensive, and the result would be a network of floating, car-like trams, that could only go where the magnetic roads were. These floating cars could not even veer off the road, let alone lift themselves away from it.

But if they can float, why can't they fly?

They cannot fly because the further apart the magnets are, the weaker the force of electromagnetic repulsion between them. In practice, electromagnets only really work over short distances – anywhere from a few centimetres to a metre. To push a maglev-car hundreds or thousands of feet into the air, you would need an immensely powerful magnet, and a massive amount of energy. It just wouldn't be worth it.

Boo. So no flying cars or anti-gravity boots for me, then.

Not flying, no. But floating, maybe. The luxury car

company Lexus has already built a **maglev hoverboard** that floats above the floor of a magnetic skatepark. In theory, you could make **maglev skates**, and zoom about in much the same way.

***Now* you're talking! Put me down for a pair of those!**

ACTIVITY:
BUILD YOUR OWN MAGLEV DEVICE

Want to see magnetic levitation in action? Then try this simple project.

You will need:

- 6 ring magnets
- 1 pencil
- 1 polystyrene block
- 1 playing card

Lay the pencil lengthwise on top of the styrofoam brick.

Push two of the ring magnets into the styrofoam brick on either side of the pencil about 2.5 cm (1 inch) from its tip.

The two other ring magnets will be placed on either side of the pencil about 2.5 cm (1 inch) from the eraser end.

Now slide the pencil through the remaining two ring magnets, and align them with the two pairs of magnets in the styrofoam.

Push a playing card into the styrofoam at the tip of the pencil. Place the pencil above the magnets in the styrofoam and watch it levitate!

WILL WE ONE DAY CONTROL COMPUTERS WITH OUR MINDS?

We already are! Whenever you give a voice command to a computer or smartphone, you are controlling a device with little more than ideas and soundwaves. There are also some experimental cyborgs in the world, who can control computers and robots with their brainwaves alone. For better or worse, the age of cybernetics is upon us.

Seriously? There will be cybernetic people one day, who can make machines do things just with their minds?

Almost certainly. If you think about it, you're already a kind of cyborg.

Eh? How's that?

The word 'cyborg' is defined like this:

> **CYBORG**: a person whose physical or mental abilities are extended beyond normal human limitations by mechanical elements built onto (or inside) the body.

In a world of voice-controlled smartphones, smartwatches, and wearable sleep, diet, and exercise trackers, we are already extending our physical and mental limits through computers and machines.

Every time you ask Siri to look up some crazy factoid on the internet, every time you

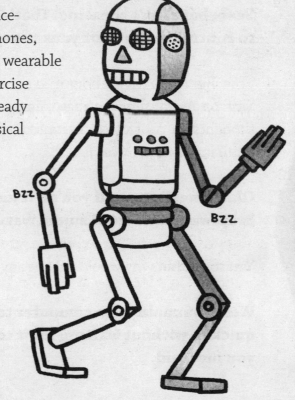

BZZ

BZZ

tap a smartwatch to view your heart rate or step count, or you use Google Maps to find an unknown place, you are interfacing with computers and using them to extend the limits of your physical senses and mental knowledge.

Granted, not everyone wants a smartphone grafted onto their skin or **implanted** inside their bodies. To be true cyborgs, that is what you would have to do. But all the same, most of us are acting like cyborgs every day.

Yeah, but that's cheating. That's using your voice to control things, not your thoughts.

True. But if you think about it, every time you shout 'Hey Siri!' or 'Alexa, find me that thing!', you are using your thoughts to control computers, you're just translating them into sound waves first.

Okay fine, But could you do it just with brainwaves, without sound waves?

You could. But why would that be any better?

Well, you could tell a computer to do things much quicker, without waiting for it to figure out what you just said.

Maybe. But in order to communicate your wishes to a computer, you would still have to organize your thoughts into specific commands. By the time you've done that, you might as well just tell it what to do. Right now, talking to computers and machines is still a little clumsy and difficult. They often mishear what we say, or misinterpret what we want.

But with constant developments in speech recognition technology, this is rapidly changing. **Apple's Siri**, **Amazon's Echo**, and other speech-activated programs are getting better and better at figuring out what we say, and what we want done. As both voice recognition and Artificial Intelligence (AI) technology continue to improve, it will not be long before we are having real conversations with computers, and figuring things out **together**.

Yeah, but it'd be so cool to control machines or play video games just with your mind. Like you could tell a robot to get something for you, or drive a car, just by thinking about it.

That's true, you could. And in fact, that kind of thought-activated technology is already in the works. There are already experimental devices that can help people with missing limbs or movement problems to **control robot**

arms and **hands**. Or to type words on a computer screen using only their brains.

Really, there are?

For years now, we have been able to attach robot arms and hands to amputees (people missing limbs from illness or accident), and wire them to the nervous system.

If the nerves in the upper arm still work, then the patient can move and grip things with their new robot arms, just by trying to flex the muscles they would have had. But if the nerves leading to the arm are damaged or lost, this does not work. Not, at least, without a brain-computer interface.

Erik Sorto is a man from California who was paralysed from the neck down by a gunshot wound. In 2015, doctors from the University of Southern California implanted a **pair of tiny microchips** into his brain, which he uses to control a **robot arm**. The chips decode his thoughts and mental commands, turn them into computer code, and transmit them to the robot arm. With practice, Erik can now use the arm to feed himself, shake hands, even play Rock, Paper, Scissors!

Since then, many more patients in the USA and China have received similar surgeries, so that they can control robot arms, motorized wheelchairs, or computer cursors using their brain alone.

So there really are cyborgs alive in the world?

Yes there are. And one day, there could be a lot more of them.

Aside from their uses and medicine and healthcare, **brain–machine interfaces** like this could one day change the way humans work, play, and communicate – perhaps forever.

Elon Musk – the billionaire founder of **SpaceX** and **Tesla** – has invested invested millions of dollars in developing **Neuralink** – the first complete brain–computer interface. The idea is to create an implantable device that would let a person **communicate directly with the internet.** In theory, this would give you instant access to a whole world of knowledge and memory, and give you the ability to control any internet-linked device.

You could control a smart home: **unlocking doors**, or turning **lights on and off** as you entered a room. You could call or text people by thought, and see their replies as thoughts and images in you head. You could drive an electric car, or control a complex video game. You could even browse and shop online.

That would be amazing! So why aren't we already doing it?

First, **Neuralink** is not yet a reality. It is just an idea. The brain–machine interfaces we have are pretty crude, and finding ways to translate brainwaves into a **coded language** that computers can understand has proven much trickier than we thought.

Second, the interface will likely have to be **in direct contact with your brain.** Which would mean **drilling a hole in your skull** to get it in there.

Okay, now that doesn't sound like fun at all . . .

Third, some scientists and engineers are worried about blurring the lines between humans and machines this way. Because if you did succeed in creating a true brain–internet interface, then the information (and control) could go both ways.

What if someone figured out how to hack the interface, getting control of your home, your bank account, or your car? Add to this the possibility of an unfriendly Artificial Intelligence (AI) and it gets even worse.

What do you mean?

Well, someday we will probably invent an Artificial Intelligence that is smarter than us. This could improve our world in unimaginable ways. But that intelligence could also decide it doesn't want to play with us. It might start working against us, actively messing up our world and its critical systems control. If those systems included all our brains, hooked up to a massive internet, then we could end up like an army of zombie cyborgs, doing whatever the Great Computer tells us!

If the AI could hack into your brain, it could control your physical movements, your heart rate and blood pressure – even your thoughts and feelings! So maybe we shouldn't be in such a rush to connect ourselves directly with our computers after all . . .

[Shudder.] I'll never look at Siri the same way again!

I'M SORRY,
I DIDN'T UNDERSTAND THAT.
DID YOU SAY:
'MAKE ME A
CYBERNETIC ZOMBIE,
IN ETERNAL SERVICE TO
THE MACHINES?'

Aaaaaaaaggghh!!! It's started!!

QUICK ONES –
ENERGY, POWER, AND MACHINES

What is the world's fastest car?

The fastest conventional petrol car to date is the **SSC Tuatara**, which has been clocked at **286 mph (460 km/h)**, and could perhaps manage **330 mph** or more. That said, it might not hold the record for long, as engineers are working on electric supercars that can hit **400 mph (643 km/h)** or more. The fastest four-wheeled vehicle ever is the **ThrustSSC**, which broke the land speed record in 1997 by reaching **763 mph (1,227 km/h)**. But given that it has two turbofan engines, it barely qualifies as a car, and is more like a jet aeroplane on wheels!

Whooosh

Why do cars crumple up in car crashes?

Car bodies are actually designed to crumple a bit during crashes, as it helps soften the shock and impact passed through to the passengers inside. When a car crashes, the front end stops suddenly, but the contents of the car (its passengers and cargo) continue moving forwards at high speed. In the early days of automobile production, cars were built far more rigidly, and passengers could be killed at even moderate speeds, as they flew through the windscreen or smashed against the dashboard, steering wheel, or engine. Adding collapsible 'crumple zones' to the front, back, and sides of the car helps to decelerate the passenger cabin and spread the force of impact around the car, so that less shock is transferred and felt. Crumple zones – along with seatbelts and crash-activated airbags – have made car travel a lot safer (though it is still one of the more dangerous forms of travel on average). You can now find crumple zones on high-speed trains, also.

How do helicopters move forwards?

Helicopters are both lifted and driven forwards by the movement of their main rotors – the twirly propellor things on top. When left in a neutral, flat position, the rotors drive air downwards, and lift the helicopter straight up. But by moving a control stick inside the cockpit, a helicopter pilot can angle the whole rotor assembly – tilting it forwards, backwards, to the left, to the right, or any direction in between. Whichever direction the rotors are tilted, they drive air in the opposite direction, pushing the helicopter in the direction of the tilt. So tilt the rotors forwards, and the aircraft moves forwards. Tilt them backwards or sideways, and the whole aircraft moves backwards or sideways. A second rotor on the tail – which balances out the lateral rotation of the main rotors – can also be used to pivot the craft left or right. The whole thing gets rather complicated, which makes flying a helicopter way harder than flying a plane!

Why aren't there more robots in houses?

Robots are difficult and expensive to build, and the kinds of things we might want them to do around the house – cooking, cleaning, folding and putting away laundry – involve quite complex movements, which are hard for robots to reproduce. House robots would also need a lot of sensors and safety features to get around safely and avoid bumping into things or accidentally injuring a human during its tasks. Robots also require a lot of energy, making them expensive to charge and run. For that reason, we are limited right now to robot hoovers and floor sweepers (like the Roomba) and voice-activated smartphone components. But over the next couple of decades, as robots become cheaper and easier to build, we may yet see robot cooks, maids, and nannies in our homes!

Could a robot ever hurt a person?

Human injuries and deaths caused by robots are quite rare, but they can and do happen. Most robot-related accidents happen in factories, where robots have been used on assembly lines since the 1980s. Robot grabbers, hammers, welders, and conveyors are dangerously powerful. But they are usually designed with safety features – like automatic 'off' switches that power down the robot when a human enters its work area.

However, humans make mistakes, and sometimes forget how dangerous (and oblivious) robots can be. The most common type of accident is a **pinch-point injury**, where a person gets pinched or squashed between a moving robot and another object. After that comes **impact injury**, where a swinging robot arm bashes someone so hard in the head or body that they die. There were at least **61** known robot-related deaths like this between 1992 and 2015. Scary as that may sound, that is only 2 or 3 robot deaths per year, compared to 2 million non-robot accidents, 18,000 of them fatal ones. So on average, less than 1 in 5,000 accidental deaths currently involve robots. That said, it will be interesting to see if that changes when self-driving cars and aircraft become more common . . .

GROWTH, HEALING, AND DISEASE

WHY ARE BRAINS ALL WRINKLY?

Not all brains are wrinkly. But the wrinkly ones happen because some layers of the brain grow faster than others, creating folds and wrinkles in its surface. Hopefully, these wrinkles create more space for connections, making big-brained animals better movers and smarter thinkers.

Hang on – do all animals even *have* brains?

Not all, but most do. Almost every kind of animal has some sort of nervous system, and most animals have a brain. The only exceptions to this rule are **sponges** and **jellyfish.** Sponges have **no nerve cells** at all, while jellyfish have a web of **nerve cells** (or **neurons)** spread out between their tentacles (rather than clustered into one blob). This makes sense, as sponges and jellyfish do not really need brains in their simple, watery lives.

Generally speaking, brains are **control centres** that help animals to **sense** and **interpret** their environment, to **move** in complex ways, and to **make decisions** about where to go and what to do. Sponges are **sessile** (or non-moving) **animals** that just sit on the seabed, absorbing food from the water. Jellyfish may bob and pulse between different depths of ocean. But they largely go where the sea currents take them.

Now compare that with an **insect**, or a **fish.** Insects and fish have more complex lives. They **graze**, **hunt**, **evade predators**, **build homes** for themselves, even **team up** and **work together** sometimes. All these things require more control and more brain power.

So as you might expect, they have the brains to accomplish them.

Do all animal brains look the same?

No they don't. They come in a wide range of shapes and sizes. But generally speaking, all animals in the same family or class have the same, basic **shape** of brain, if not the same **size**. So while a **great white shark** has a much bigger brain than a **clownfish**, their brains have the same basic shape and appearance. This makes sense, since for all their differences they are still both fish. They live in the same ocean environments, and move their bodies in similar ways to get around.

Reptiles, such as snakes and tortoises, have brains with similar shapes, too. As do the **insect** brains of flies and beetles, and the **mammalian** brains of bats and beavers. The biggest difference in brain shape is between **vertebrate animals** (like fish and field mice) and **invertebrate animals** (like spiders and lobsters).

How's that?

All vertebrates have at least **three** separate layers of the brain. This includes lower **brainstem**, an inner **limbic system**, and an outer **cerebral cortex**. The **brainstem** controls basic life support (like breathing and body temperature), while the **limbic system** supplies **feelings**, **emotions**, and emergency **fight-or-flight** responses.

But the vertebrate **cerebral cortex** is where all the truly **clever** stuff happens. This includes the co-ordination of **complex movements**, like running, climbing, and using tools. And in humans, it also includes areas for **speech**, **language**, **logic**, **planning**, **imagination**, and **self control**.

As you might imagine, **bigger, cleverer animals** have **bigger, thicker cortexes**.

Whales, dolphins, gorillas, and humans have a thick cortex. Mice, squirrels, and lizards do not. And tellingly, the brains of big, clever animals have **more folds and wrinkles** in the outer cortex, while **smaller, simpler** animals have **smooth surfaces** to their brains.

So not all brains are wrinkly?

Nope. Most animal brains are smooth. Only **higher mammals** have wrinkled surfaces to their brains. Neuroscientists (doctors and scientists who study brains) have special names for these folds and wrinkles: the folds and bumps are called **gyri**, while the grooves and valleys between the folds are called **sulci**. The bigger the brain, the more gyri and sulci it has.

So what are the folds actually for?

Good question. We know how the wrinkles and folds **get there**, but we are not yet certain of everything they do. We know that big brains get wrinkly because two different types of tissue within the brain grow at different rates.

There are two basic types of tissue in the brain: **grey matter** and **white matter**. **Grey matter** is more densely packed with cells and blood vessels, giving it a **pinkish-grey** colour. **White matter** has fewer cells, but more **axons** – which are like the electrical cables carrying signals from one area of the brain to another. These axons are coated with a yellowish-white protein called **myelin**, to speed up signal flow along the cable. This myelin gives white matter its milky colour and density.

As it turns out, **grey matter grows faster than white matter** during brain development. So in big brains with a thick cortex layer, the grey matter bunches up, folding the slower-growing white matter around it, and creating deep wrinkles and folds in the cortex. In smaller brains, (less than three centimetres across) this difference in growth rate doesn't have much of an effect, so the cortex stays smooth. This is why **mice** and **squirrels** have smooth brains, while **elephants**, **whales**, and **humans** have wrinkly ones.

So is that also why elephants and humans are cleverer than squirrels? Because we have thicker brains with more wrinkles in them?

That is probably a big part of it, yes. Having **more wrinkles** allows us to pack **more neurons** (or brain cells) into the outermost layers of our brain. The wrinkles also create a **wider surface area** within which those cells can **connect** to each other.

Having a more complex **network of connections** is probably what allows us to make more **complex movements** – like **holding and carrying things with a trunk, throwing rocks, making tools,** or **firing a bow and arrow** at a moving target. But it also seems like having more connections increases our ability to **learn, remember, think, plan,** and **ponder different outcomes** to our actions.

So you can thank your wrinkles for both **how agile** and **how clever** you are. It is thanks to your big brain, thick cortex, and deep wrinkles that you can **somersault, skateboard, speak, sing,** and **solve tricky maths problems**.

Cool! Wish I had the trunk, though. I would trade that for maths skills any day.

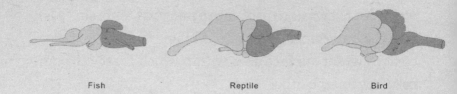

Fish   Reptile   Bird

AMAZING BRAINS

● Spiders have extremely large brains for their size. Some spider's brains occupy more than 80% of their body – spilling out of their heads and into their abdomens and legs. Big brains help them with hunting, web building, and complex movements unique to spiders.

● Sea squirts are sea creatures that look like tadpoles as young animals, then anchor onto the sea floor to live motionless as adults. The first thing they do after anchoring is eat their own brain – as they no longer need it for movement.

● Human brains triple in size between birth and 1 year of age. They keep growing until you are around 18 years old.

Mammal

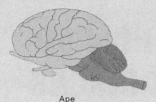
Ape

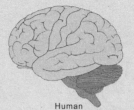
Human

- There are no pain receptors in the brain, which means that brain surgeons can sometimes prod around and remove tumours while the patient is still wide awake (though they still need local anaesthetics to numb the scalp and skull).

- At any given time, your brain is using around 20% of the blood and oxygen in your body. When you are deep in thought, that may rise to 50% or more.

- While you are awake, your brain generates about 1–25 watts of electricity – enough to power a small light bulb.

HOW DO POISONS WORK?

There are thousands of poisons in the world, and they can work in lots of different ways. Some are swallowed or breathed in. Others are injected or absorbed through the skin. The one thing all poisons have in common is this: they mess with our organs and essential body systems. Some of them in ways that are hard to reverse.

Where do poisons come from?

The oldest and best-known poisons come from living things – including **plants**, **bacteria**, **fungi**, or **animals** (especially fish, frogs, and octopuses). Many plants and animals create poisons and toxins for attack and defence. Some bacteria, meanwhile, contain toxins in their bodies, which damage animal cells and tissues if they are attacked by immune cells and split open.

Is there any difference between a poison and a toxin? Is one worse than the other?

The words *poison* and *toxin* describe similar, but slightly different things.

Generally speaking, a **poison** is a naturally occurring substance, made by living organisms, which **does harm** if it is **swallowed**, **inhaled** or **absorbed**.

A **toxin** is **any kind of harmful substance** that does damage to the human body. This includes natural biological **poisons** (sometimes called **biotoxins**), but also dangerous man-made chemicals like **Sarin** and **VX gas**. In short, **all poisons are toxins**, but **not all toxins are poisons**.

What's a venom, then?

A **venom** is a specific type of **biotoxin** produced by an animal – typically a snake, spider, or stinging insect – which is **injected** into its victim by **biting** or **stinging**.

Technically, **rattlesnakes** are **venomous** (since they inject you with toxins), but not **poisonous** (since you can actually eat one, without suffering harm). Fly agaric mushrooms, on the other hand, are **poisonous** (since they can kill you if you eat them), but not **venomous** (as they do not bite or sting). Make sense?

Okay, got it. So how do poisons work?

There are literally thousands of poisons and toxins in the world, and they work in lots of different ways. **Toxicologists** – scientists who study poisons and toxins – put them into groups based on **where they come from.**

There are **biological toxins** and **poisons** – which are proteins made inside living organisms – and there are **chemical** or **physical poisons** like cyanide or polonium.

You can then put toxins into smaller groups, based on how they do damage.

Haemotoxins attack blood cells, causing death by blood clot, out-of-control bleeding, or the destruction of blood cells. Many deadly **snake venoms** are haemotoxins.

Myotoxins attack muscle tissue, paralysing or damaging your muscles, and leaving you unable to move or breathe. Some jellyfish stings are myotoxins.

Necrotoxins destroy cells en masse, eating into tissues and organs, and leaving gaping holes in your body. Some spider toxins, like those of the **black widow** and **brown recluse** spider are necrotoxins.

Neurotoxins are perhaps the deadliest type of all. They attack your brain or nervous system – jamming signals or making them fire like crazy. Some neurotoxins prevent you from sending signals to your muscles, causing death by **paralysis** and **suffocation**. Others stop your **heart** or make the **brain** shut down. Neurotoxins can be found in certain **spiders** (funnel- web spiders) **snakes** (kraits, cobras, black mambas), **scorpions**, **wasps**, and **sea anemones**. Some neurotoxins (like those of wasps) just cause pain and temporary numbness. Others can cause death within minutes.

Yikes. So what's the deadliest poison there is?

The deadliest poison we know of is called **botulinum toxin,** which is a neurotoxin made by the bacterium *Clostridium botulinum*. These bacteria can lurk in uncooked meat, causing a severe form of food poisoning called **botulism**. This toxin is so deadly that just a **thousandth of a gram** of it (the same as two grains of salt) is enough to kill a **fully grown elephant**.

Close second is **batrachotoxin**, made by the deadly

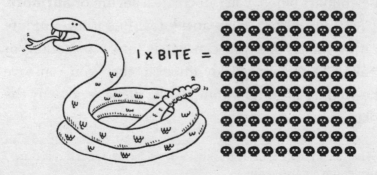

I x BITE =

poison arrow frogs of Central and South America. This toxin attacks nerve cells, resulting in paralysis and rapid death. Native tribes in South America have been dipping their arrows and blowdart into the skins of poison arrow frogs for thousands of years – making them lethal with a single scratch. Batrachotoxin is all the more dangerous because there is no known **antidote**.

Okay – last question – what actually is an antidote?

An **antidote** is a substance that counteracts a specific toxin. Antidotes are usually made by injecting a tiny amount of a toxin into a big, healthy animal – like a pig or a sheep.

A healthy animal will then create **antibodies** in its blood – proteins that bind to that specific type of toxin and deactivated it. By drawing these antibodies out of the animal's blood, you can create a **serum** or **antidote**.

Not all poisons have antidotes. But if an antidote can be made, and you can get it into a poisoning or snake-bite victim[*] quickly enough, then you can save the victim's life, and minimize the damage done by the toxin.

....

[*] When an antidote is made to a snake or spider venom, it is called an **antivenom**, or **antivenin**.

[Shudder.] Poisons are *scary*.

They are indeed. But some poisons and toxins have positive uses, too.

Warfarin, a kind of rat poison that stops blood cells from clotting, is used in the treatment of heart conditions, by preventing deadly blood clots after surgery. **Pit-viper venom** can be used to treat high blood pressure – extending the life of sufferers by many years. The same substance can kill you or help you. It all depends on how much you use.

Toxicologists like to say: **everything is toxic in a high enough dose**. And in small doses, **a little bit of what kills you really can make you stronger**.

Just don't go testing that on yourself. Leave those venomous snakes and spiders alone.

Don't worry – I will!

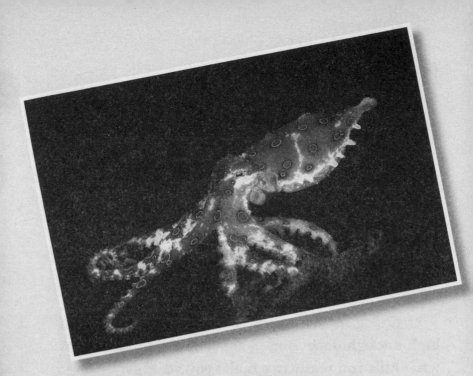

DEADLY VENOMS AND TOXINS

● The **Belcher's sea snake** is more dangerous than 95% of the snakes on land. Its bite can kill an adult human in under 30 minutes. But like most snakes, they are shy and rarely bite unless provoked.

● The **deathstalker scorpion** not only has the coolest name of all arachnids, it is also responsible for more than three quarters of all scorpion-related deaths each year. Its sting paralyses your lungs, filling them with fluid, in which you drown. Yikes.

- The **box jellyfish** has killed over 5,500 people worldwide since 1954. Its stinging tentacles contain tiny, venom-filled harpoons, which attack the heart and nervous system. Australians know to give them a wide berth when swimming and scuba-diving.

- The **blue-ringed octopus** is as beautiful as it is deadly. Although small, a single animal contains enough venom to kill 25 people. The venom attacks the nervous system and stops you breathing within minutes.

- The **puffer fish** inflates when threatened, deterring predators looking to eat it. If that doesn't work, its liver produces a poison called tetrodotoxin, which is 1,200 times more poisonous than cyanide, and to which there is no known antidote.

- The **inland taipan** snake lives in central Australia, and has one of the most toxic venoms in the world. A single drop of its venom can kill 100 adult humans, and causes both paralysis and internal bleeding. Thankfully, it is so shy – and lives in such a remote area – that the average number of deaths it causes each year is zero.

DOES EVERYONE SEE THE SAME COLOURS?

Most humans see the same wavelengths of light, which we label as colours in the brain. But not everyone can tell the difference between reds and greens, or shades of blue and yellow – meaning that some people really are 'blind' to certain colours. Then again, some people can see millions more colours than you can.

Some people really can't see colours at all? They just see in black and white?

Total colour blindness (or **monochromia)** in humans is rare, but it can happen. People with **monochromia** really do just see the world in black and white, with shades of grey in between. But far more often, so-called 'colour-blind' people can see some colours but not all of them. Or rather, their eyes detect all colour of light, but some appear muted or flattened out, making it hard to tell the difference between, say, different shades of red, or different shades of green.

How does that even happen?

Light travels in waves, and colours are actually **waves of light** within different **patterns** or **wavelengths**. One wave pattern we see as **red**, another as **yellow**, and so on.

The ability to see **all** of these wave patterns is actually quite rare in the animal kingdom. Most animals see in black and white (**monochrome**) or in shades of **one or two colours only** (**duochrome**). This is because not all animals have the necessary **detectors** to pick up all the wave patterns and communicate them to the brain.

So what are the wave detectors – eyeballs?

Correct. But not all animal eyeballs contain the same parts.

Most have a **pupil** to let in light, a **lens** to focus that light, and a screen (or **retina**) at the back of the eyeball, on which that light is focused.

The **retina** contains two major types of light-sensing cell: **rod cells** and **cone cells**.

Rods can detect the **presence** or **absence** of light, but cannot tell the difference between different **wavelengths** (or **colours**) of light. These rod cells work by day and by night, provided there is at least a little bit of moonlight or candlelight around.

Cone cells, however, can detect different wavelengths and colours[*]. They are triggered by **bands** of light in certain wavelengths. One type of cone cell (S-cones) detects blue wavelengths. Another (M-cones) detects green wavelengths, and a third (L-cones) detects red

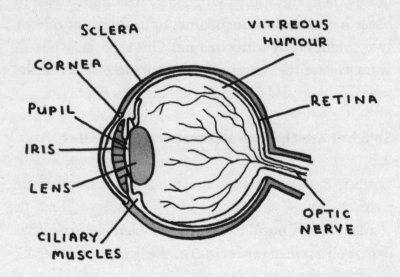

SCLERA

CORNEA

PUPIL

IRIS

LENS

CILIARY MUSCLES

VITREOUS HUMOUR

RETINA

OPTIC NERVE

---

[*] Cones require more light than rods, though, and do not work well in low light. This is why colours are impossible to see in near-darkness – only fuzzy shades of grey.

wavelengths. If an animal has **all three** types of cone cell, then it can detect all the colours of the rainbow – **red**, **green**, **blue**, and everything in between.

Roughly **92%** of humans have **all three** types of cone cell, so they see in full colour. The same goes for most other primates, like **lemurs**, **gorillas**, and **chimpanzees**.

But **cats**, **dogs** and **squirrels** are missing one type of cone cell – the red-sensing L-cone. Which means they see in shades of blue and green, but cannot see red – or at least the wavelength of light we would recognize as 'red'*.

So are colour-blind people missing cone cells, too?

Very few colour-blind people lack cone cells altogether, and cannot see any colours at all. The vast majority of colour-blind people are not 'blind' to colours at all. Rather, they have cone cells that are altered and a little less sensitive to certain wavelengths than they should be. So they can see colours – just a little less vividly. And to them, the difference between certain pairs of colours is less obvious.

....

* They do, however, have reflective retinas, which lets them see in the dark much better than we do. So it's not all bad being a feline or canine!

Are there lots of colour-blind people in the world?

More than you might think. In the United Kingdom, around 3 million people (or 5% of the population) are colour-blind. Worldwide, there are about **300 million** people with some form of colour blindness – which is about as many people as there are living in the entire United States of America!

For various reasons, colour blindess is more common in boys than girls. About 1 in 12 men is colour-blind, compared to 1 in 200 women.

What's it actually *like* to be colour-blind? What does the world look like to all those people?

That depends what form of colour blindness you have. The most common is a form of red-green colour blindness called **deuteranomaly**, in which the **green cone cells** function abnormally. For people with **deuteranomaly**, **blues** and **purples** are easily mixed up, and yellows and greens seem redder than they should. To them, a bright yellow banana might look somewhat **orange**.

Another form of red-green colour blindness is called **protanomaly**. Here, the **red cone cells** are damaged. This means that **reds**, **oranges** and **yellows** look a bit

greener than normal. To someone with this condition, a **bright red apple** would appear **dull green** instead. So you might mix up your Cox apples with your Granny Smiths, but there's nothing too drastic about that. More rarely, we find colour-blind people whose **red** or **green cone cells** do not work at all. This is called **protanopia**, and people with this condition may see a red apple as **black** or **grey**.

Slightly less common than **red-green** colour blindness is blue-yellow colour blindness.

Most people with this condition simply have **fewer blue cone cells** than they should in their retinas, meaning that **blues** are easily mistaken for **greens**. Interestingly, this is common in **Japan**, where for thousands of years there was no specific word in the language for **green***, and people still describe blue **sky** and green **grass** using the same colour word – aoi.

That's wild! I can't imagine not being able to see the colours I see now.

Well, unless you had the ability to see them, then lost it, you wouldn't know what you were missing. Colour blindness can develop later in life as we age, or in

* Japanese people do have a specific word for the colour green – *midori*. But they still use *aoi* for blue or green.

response to certain diseases or drugs. But most people are **born** with it, and many do not even notice they are colour-blind, unless someone points it out to them.

Besides, there are people and animals in the world who can see millions of colours that you cannot.

There are?!

Yep, so called **tetrachromats** have not three, but **four** types of cone cell in their retinas. This means they can see wavelengths of light beyond the normal human range – including invisible ultraviolet and infrared wavelengths. They can distinguish between perhaps thousands of colours that you and I would see as identical.

Many **birds** are **tetrachromats**, as are some **fish** and **insects**. This means they can see ultraviolet patterns on **feathers**, **leaves**, and **corals** that are invisible to most humans.

Some **monkeys** are tetrachromats, too – seeing countless shades of **orange** and **yellow** that our eyes cannot. This is helpful for spotting **fruit** in a dense forest canopy.

What about people?

We do not know exactly how many human tetrachromats

there are in the world. But scientists guess that perhaps 1% of all women (they are almost always women) may be tetrachromats worldwide. That means there are nearly **80 million** people who can see **100 million times** as many colours as you can.

As you might expect, many of these people become **fine artists**, **decorators** and **designers**.

100 million times as many colours? Wow! Now I'm jealous!

Well, who knows – in the future, we may find a way to **genetically engineer** our eyeballs, so that we are **all** tetrachromats. Then we could all enjoy a brighter, more vibrant view of daily life. We may even alter our cone cells to pick up **infrared heat trails** in complete darkness.

Okay, now I definitely want *that* . . .

ACTIVITY: DECODING COLOURS

This colour experiment looks at the absorption of light through a part of your eye called the **retina,** and the decoding of colours through **cone cells**.

You will need:

● A drawing or print out of an object (a star, heart or other shape) that has a yellow border, a green interior and a small black dot in the centre

● A blank sheet of white paper with only a small black dot in the centre

● A few blank white sheets of paper

● Markers to draw your own images

Stare at the yellow and green image for 20 seconds, focusing on the small black dot in the centre of the picture. Then immediately look at the blank sheet of paper focusing on the small black dot.

What do you see? What happened to the border and interior of the image?

Why do you think this happened? What colours does the brain group together?

To continue the experiment, you can make drawings of other shapes or images with yellow and blue together, or red and green.

What happens if you simply reverse the yellow border and green interior? Examine your results, and what you can figure out about your eyeballs!

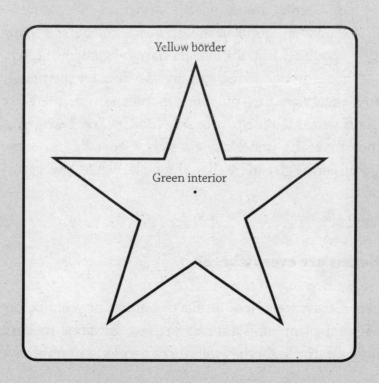

Yellow border

Green interior

WHAT MAKES SOME GERMS GOOD AND OTHER GERMS BAD?

Germs live almost everywhere in nature – underground, in the air, inside and outside living bodies. Most of them are harmless, and just hitch-hike through living systems, feeding on the matter and energy we cast off. But among the rest, there are 'good' germs that help us to stay healthy, and 'bad' germs that make us unhealthy or sick. Generally speaking, 'good' germs give more than they take, while 'bad' germs do the opposite.

Germs are everywhere?

Yep. Germs were here on Earth billions of years before the first plants and animals arrived, let alone modern humans. No doubt they will still be here long after we have gone. They live in every conceivable nook and cranny of our world, from the deepest oceans and jungles, to the air we breathe and the ground beneath our feet. They live **on or inside every living thing on the planet** – including you and me.

What are germs anyway?

Germs, also known as **microbes**, are tiny microscopic organisms, smaller than the head of a pin. Many germs are **bacteria** – single-celled life forms that come in a wide range of microscopic shapes and sizes. Some are rod-shaped (**bacilli**), others are blob-like (**cocci**), and still others are like tiny spirals of pasta (**spirilla**).

Other germs include **protists** – single-celled organisms that are typically a bit larger and more complicated than bacteria – and **viruses**.

Viruses are **tiny parasites** that jump from cell to cell, hijack the DNA within to copy and spread themselves to new hosts. Scientists do not all agree on whether viruses are alive, since they cannot grow or reproduce without help. But regardless, they are found inside all living things, so have a massive impact on health and survival.

How many kinds of bacteria are there?

There are millions of species of bacteria on Earth, and we have probably only discovered about 1% of them. Some of the more common ones are **staphylococci** which live on the surface of your skin, **streptococci** which live in your mouth and throat, and **lactobacilli** which live in your gut.

We have germs in our mouth and guts? All the time?

Yep, in your mouth, in your stomach, in your guts, up your bum. All day, every day. No one is entirely germ-free. In fact, if you count up the total number of bacterial cells hitch-hiking inside and upon your body, they **outnumber your own body cells ten to one!** In other words, your body is a living, breathing **colony of organisms** which is only about **10% human**.

Okay, that's just weird. So if they're in us and on us all day, how come we don't get sick all the time?

Because most bacteria are **harmless** to our health, and our bodies have learned to live happily with them for thousands of years. Some are even **helpful** to us, performing functions that we cannot do without them. The **lactobacilli** in your gut, for example, help kids to digest **lactose** – a kind of sugar found in milk – which humans have trouble breaking down. **Lactobacilli,** along with thousands of other bacterial species, are passed to you by your mother – swallowed on the way out of the womb, or taken in through breast milk in your first year of life.

Other gut microbes like **Bifidobacteria, Streptococcus thermophilus**, and **Saccharomyces boulardii**, help us to **absorb critical vitamins and nutrients**, **reduce gas and bloating (i.e fart production)**, and help **keep your poo solid** (as opposed to liquid, which nobody enjoys).

Similarly helpful microbes line your airways and

lungs, your teeth and gums, and every possible crevice of your skin. Some do little of anything besides hitch-hike, but at the very least their presence protects against invading hordes of 'bad' microbes, which can do damage.

Aha! So there are bad bacteria!

Yes, there are. Some microbes are harmful **parasites**. They take more from us than they give, and do harm to our body systems in the process.

These include bacteria like *Campylobacter* and *Salmonella*, which enter our bodies in dodgy uncooked food. When these bad boys set up shop in your stomach or gut, they wreak havoc on your digestion. The result is **food poisoning**, and hours or days of vomiting, stomach cramps, and or runny poo. Some, like the *Clostridium botulinum* bacterium that causes **botulism**, can even be lethal.

Do all bad germs get in through food?

Not all of them no. Some are transmitted from your hands to your mouth after you touch an infected surface or body fluid. These include **Norovirus**, which causes non-stop vomiting, and harmful strains of *E.coli*. *E.coli* actually live in your gut all the time. But when they travel from bum to mouth, they can cause serious problems.

Other germs enter the body through cuts or punctures in your skin.

Skin forms a **natural barrier** to harmful bugs. But when an opening appears, bugs like *Staphylococcus aureus* (which live harmlessly on the outside of your skin) can do massive damage once they get underneath it.

This points out an interesting fact – many bacteria are neither good nor bad. They are more like friends that you invite to your house for a party. Most of the time, they behave themselves well and everybody has a good time. But if left unsupervised for too long, they can misbehave, party too hard, and do serious damage to their surroundings.

Some **bacterial infections** are caused by nasty, rare, exotic bugs that always cause trouble. But most, perhaps, are caused by **everyday bacteria** that end up in the **wrong place** in your body. They are not **trying** to harm you. They just **do**.

Together, the sum total of microbes living on and within your body is called your **microbiome**. And depending on what you **eat**, where you **live**, and how you **behave**, your microbiome might be healthy (filled with mostly good bacteria in the proper places) or unhealthy (filled with bad bacteria in the wrong places, and causing trouble).

Since your body contains more bacterial cells than it does human ones, your microbiome can make a huge difference to how healthy you look and feel.

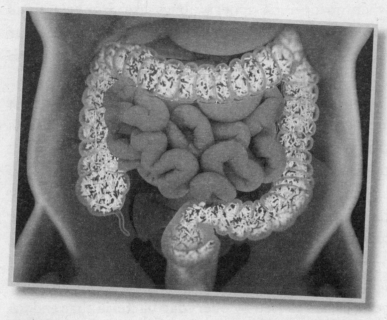

So how can we protect ourselves against the bad ones but keep the good ones in place?

An excellent question. One major way is by controlling which ones get to **enter** your body. You can keep out the bad germs – and stop good ones going where they should not – by washing your hands **before you eat** and **after you go to the toilet**. Then wherever possible, avoid getting other people's fluids (spit, vomit or poo) on you, as these fluids are teeming with bacteria that someone else was trying to get out of their body!

Cleaning and protecting **cuts**, **scrapes** and **burns** is also very important. During the terrible wars of the late 19th and early 20th century, soldiers would lose entire **limbs** to cuts and wounds infected by soil bacteria in the trenches. Even now, cuts from old rusty nails or dirty metal objects can carry deadly **tetanus** bacteria through your skin*. But by cleaning a cut with soapy water and antiseptic cream, and covering it with a clean bandage or plaster, you can keep the bad bugs out until the skin has a chance to regenerate, sealing the breech.

That said, it's important to balance this cleanliness and hygiene with a good amount of **exposure** to bacteria and outdoor environments. If you try to keep your house and body **too clean**, especially with the use of **antibiotics**, then you could kill off all the good bacteria living in your skin and gut, creating openings for the bad ones to colonize you.

Worse yet, if your immune system is not used

---

* That's why it's also a good idea to get a tetanus vaccine injection, if you get a cut like this.

to encountering lots of bacteria regularly, it can **overreact** when even good bacteria get into your body, creating **allergic reactions** like **asthma**, **hay fever**, and **dust allergies**. You need to create a **balance** between getting **good and dirty** and keeping your eating habits, toilet habits, cuts and scrapes **hygienic**.

Is that it, then? Get dirty, but wash your hands afterwards?

You can also control your gut microbiome through **diet** – by feeding the good bacteria, and trying not to feed the bad ones. If you want to build up a healthy variety of good bacteria in your gut, you can eat **prebiotic** and **probiotic** foods. These put good bacteria into your body, and help them to grow and colonize free spaces. Prebiotic foods include **garlic**, **onions**, **oats**, **leeks,** and **asparagus.** Probiotic foods include **yogurt**, **kimchi**, **miso paste** and **sauerkraut**.

At the same time, avoid giving the 'bad boys' too much to chow down on. Fed too much of what they like, some 'bad' bacteria can grow out of control and take over your whole gut. You will find this out if you eat too many **fermentable foods** (like **honey**, **jam**, **fruit juices** and **processed sugars**) or too much **deep fried**,

fatty, and **processed meat** (the kind you find in fast food restaurants).

No fair! Burgers, fried chicken, and sugary sweets are so yum!

True. But the bad bugs think so, too. So unless you want them to take over your body, you should keep that stuff to a minimum. As in 'rare treat', not 'every day for dinner'.

Remember, you're only 10% human as it is . . .

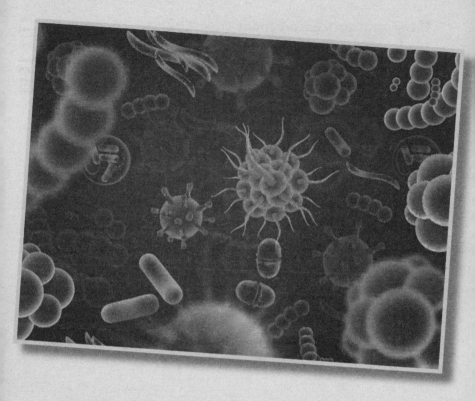

GERMS AND MICROBES

● There are more microbes in a single human body than there are stars in our galaxy.

● The combined weight of all your microbes is about three pounds (1.4 kg) – roughly the same weight as your brain. 99% of them live in your gut.

- You are born more or less bacteria-free. It is only during and after birth that microbes from your mother (and the air around you) colonize your skin, enter your mouth and nose, and set up shop inside your lungs and guts. Breast milk contains unique nutrients that help the 'good' bacteria to get a foothold before the 'bad' ones can.

- Microbes in your skin – especially your hands, feet, armpits, and groin – are constantly battling fungal spores. This protects you against fungal infections like Athlete's Foot.

- Antibiotics can help you fight dangerous bacterial infections. But when overused, they can also kill off colonies of 'good' bacteria, leaving you vulnerable to lung infections, gut problems, and weight gain.

- Right now, at least 1,200 species of bacteria are living in your mouth. This is regardless of how well you brushed your teeth this morning (although not brushing lets the nasty ones grow faster). The foul-smelling sulphurous chemicals they produce create the 'morning breath' you wake up with. Trust me – this gets worse with age.

WHY CAN'T WE REGROW DAMAGED ORGANS?

Some human tissues and organs – like the liver – can and do regrow naturally, without any help from doctors. But some human tissues do not, and have to be removed or replaced if they are damaged. But scientists and doctors are already working on ways to regrow and regenerate damaged organs – both inside and outside our bodies.

So, some organs *do* regrow themselves?

Yes. In fact, many organs and tissues do, every day. **Skin** is technically the largest organ in your body, and skin is **constantly** repairing and regrowing itself. Even when· you are not accidentally **scraping**, **burning**, or **puncturing** it, your skin falls off all by itself – leaving tiny traces of you everywhere you go. Your skin regenerates fully once every 28 days. In other words, you are kind of like a snake that sheds its skin, slowly, over the course of a month.

Ewwww.

The lining of your gut regrows itself, just as enthusiastically as your skin does. Your gut lining sheds and replaces itself every two to four weeks, with parts of it **slipping out with every poo you do.**[*]

Double ewwwww. So why doesn't everything regrow like that? Like, hearts, brains, and livers, too?

Scientists have been trying to answer that question for at least a century. Part of the answer came fifty years ago, with the discovery of **stem cells** in blood and other tissues.

As you know, the entire body is made of cells, and there are many different **cell types** in the body. These include **muscle cells**, **blood cells**, **bone cells**, **nerve cells**, **skin cells**, and **liver cells** – to name just a few. These cells assemble themselves into layers and clumps

....
[*] One reason to eat a diet rich with plant fibres is that it helps scrape the gut clean of these shedding layers, making space for newer, healthier tissues.

267

called **tissues** (like muscle tissue, skin tissue, and liver tissue). Tissues, in turn, fold themselves into **organs** (entire muscles, bones, kidneys, and livers). But if you think about it, at some point, these were all just **one type of cell** – a fertilized egg cell lurking in your mother's womb.

As an animal embryo grows and develops, these cells divide, multiply, and mature into specific cell types, which migrate to different parts of the embryo. Along the way, they become **stem cells** – cells that can mature into **one or many types of tissue**.

Some of these stem cells remain in your tissues and organs for life, even after you are fully grown. But not all tissues and organs contain many stem cells.

Your **blood**, **guts**, and **skin** contain oodles of stem cells, so they can spawn fresh cells very rapidly, and repair themselves quickly if damaged. Your **liver** contains lots of stem cells, too, and can regenerate rapidly after after damage (by disease or poisoning).

Other tissues and organs, though, contain very few stem cells, and regrow very slowly, if at all. These include **nervous tissue**, **brain tissue** and **cardiac** (or heart) **muscle**.

This is why it is much easier to heal from **cuts**, **bruises**, and **blood loss** than it is to recover from **heart conditions** or **brain diseases**.

But if the liver has lots of stem cells, why do people still die of liver diseases?

Because sometimes the liver becomes damaged **faster than it can repair itself.**

The same goes for **skin**, **blood** and other regenerative organs. If you suffer **burns** on 100% of your skin at once, or **lose too much blood** all in one go, then your stem cells cannot regenerate quickly enough. If that happens, then your only choice is to **transplant** skin, blood, kidneys, lungs, hearts or livers from somebody else.

Unfortunately, transplants are not always available and do not always succeed.

Blood, liver, and lung donors can be hard to find. Even when they are available, your body may **reject** a transplanted organ if the donor's organs look too different from your own.

For this reason, doctors and scientists have been exploring the idea of **regenerative medicine** – that is replacing or regrowing damaged organs – more and more in the last few decades.

Can we really do that? How does it work?

There are three major ideas in regenerative medicine. The main one is **tissue engineering**. This uses **adult**

stem cells (sometimes from the patient's own body, sometimes donated by somebody else) and special **biomaterials** to regrow entire organs – either inside or outside the body.

Stem cells are amazing, but they don't always grow the way we want them to. You can grow stem cells in a flat dish, and they multiply happily to form a solid layer of heart, liver or kidney tissue, without complaint. But when you try to make them grow in three dimensional shapes, they tend to shrivel and die. This is because real hearts, livers, and kidneys have a three-dimensional structure, complete with scaffolds that organize the cells, and blood vessels for supplying nutrients and clearing out wastes. So to get around this, scientists have to use special **biomaterials** to create an **artificial scaffold** for the stem cells, and encourage these cells to grow on **that**. This done, you can transplant the whole organ into the body, as you would a donated one.

Does that work?

Yep – it can and does work. We have already had success with lab-grown **skin**, **oesophaguses** (food tubes), and even parts of a **lung**, **liver** and **kidney.** In years to come, we may be able to regrow and implant entire organs this way.

Crazy. So what are the other ideas?

The other two approaches are **stem cell therapy** and **artificial organs**.

Stem cell therapy involves taking **special**, **super-adaptable stem cells** and injecting them **directly** into damaged organs and tissues. So far, this seems to work pretty well for **damaged muscles** and **joints**, but less well for **damaged nerves** and **brains**. But again, we could soon have major breakthroughs here too.

In the meantime, a third group of scientists is busy building **artificial hearts**, **lungs** and **kidneys** out of non-biological plastics and metals. Some of these have weird and crazy shapes that look nothing like normal organs. Yet they seem to function well enough to keep people alive for months or years.

One artificial heart has whirring, screw-like propellers that drive a continuous flow of blood, but with no heartbeat! Who knows, maybe one day we will improve on nature's design, and implant **super hearts**, **super lungs** and **super livers**. Eventually, people with heart, lung and liver diseases may become stronger and fitter than the rest of us.

Yes! Bionic organs! This is *exactly* how we get to cyborg superheroes!

QUICK ONES –
ORGANS, AGEING, AND DISEASES

Why does skin go wrinkly when we get old?

Skin goes wrinkly because it becomes less firm and less elastic as we age.

Young skin looks (and feels) smooth and tight because it contains a good balance of two important proteins – **elastin** (which makes skin stretchy, or elastic) and **collagen** (which makes skin firm and tight). Right up to age 20, your body makes ample supplies of both of these. But from then on, it makes less and less elastin and collagen every year. As the years roll by, your skin becomes softer, looser, and fails to recoil when stretched – like an old elastic band. Skin starts to

crumple and fold, sag under gravity, hang off your bones and muscles. A good diet can help slow this process down, but you cannot stop it altogether. Some people try to erase wrinkles with collagen creams or facelifts (surgeries to stretch the skin out again). And that can work for a time. But sooner or later, we all become old wrinklies. (Me – I look at wrinkles like tiny badges of honour – awards for having lived another year.)

Why do you get more diseases as you get older?

The human body is constantly growing, repairing itself, and fighting off viruses and bacteria. But all of these abilities become slower and weaker with age. From age 30 onwards, your body's ability to repair itself – and to fight off nasty infections – becomes less and less each year, making you more likely to succumb to diseases like pneumonia and the flu. The DNA in your cells, which copies itself every time a cell grows and divides, also becomes more garbled and error-ridden over time. This can lead to partly-inherited diseases like heart disease, kidney disease, and cancer. Even eating and breathing create damage to your cells over time, wearing everything down faster than your body can repair it. This is why you should eat as much fresh food, and get as much clean air and exercise, as you can. We can't stop ageing or age-related diseases (at least not yet). But we can slow them down by making healthier choices.

Could you ever get a brain transplant?

You can transplant a heart, you can transplant a lung, and you can transplant a liver. But you cannot transplant a head or brain – at least not with our current medical knowledge and technology. This is partly because your brain is so much more complicated than other organs, and partly because we have no way of keeping one functioning (or alive) once you remove it from a body. Hearts, lungs, and livers can be cooled down to reduce their need for blood and oxygen, buying time for surgeons to remove them from a (recently-deceased) donor and hook them up to the recipient's blood supply and nervous system. But brains need a constant supply of blood and oxygen to keep working, and even a few minutes without them can lead to shutdown and brain death. Even the fastest transplant operations take hours, rather than minutes.

So the donor's brain would be dead before you could get it into a new body. It is possible that in the future we might design machines that could keep brains alive outside the body – perhaps sitting in a liquid tank, bathed in nutrients and fed oxygen through artificial blood vessels. But for now at least, brain swaps are off the menu.

Why do we only have hair on our heads (and not everywhere else)?

A good question. Of the 6,000 or so mammals on this planet, humans are one of very few species that doesn't have thick hair (or fur) all over their bodies. Early humans (or hominids) were a lot more ape like, and did have thick hair all over their bodies. These pre-human ancestors, who lived millions of years ago, spent most of their time in the shady forests and mountains of Africa, hunting, gathering, and eating plant roots, just as modern gorillas do. But around 3 million years ago, the global climate started to cool. This turned African forests into grasslands (or savannahs), and exposed our hairy ancestors to more direct sunlight.

So rather than swelter to death, our ancestors gradually thinned out their body hair – making it thinner, shorter, and wispier – and evolved more sweat glands to cool off their bare skin by evaporation. We kept thick hair on our heads, though, to serve as brain-shades (think hairy baseball cap), and to demonstrate how young and healthy we are to partners and mates. (If your hair starts thinning or falling out, then you are either getting sick or getting old – both of which make you less attractive choices for having babies with.) This is probably why we make such a big deal of judging people's attractiveness by their hairstyle even now. Which is kind of weird, if you think about it . . .

Why do kids look like their parents?

What you look like – face shape, eye colour, hair colour, skin tone – is largely programmed by your DNA. DNA is found in every cell, and forms the blueprint for how your face (and everything else) develops – from when you were in the womb, through birth, and on into adulthood. You get exactly half your DNA from your mother, and the other half from your father. These two halves first meet when the egg and sperm cell that made you get together. Although there is a little blending and exchange, the two blueprints – one from mum, one from dad – stay largely unchanged throughout life. Each blueprint contributes some instructions towards building your total face and body shape. Some instructions (and shapes) are stronger than others – which is why you may end up with your mother's nose shape, but your father's ears or jawline. But generally speaking, kids look like a mixture of their parents, with some obvious 'mum' features, and 'dad' features dominating elsewhere. Of course, this doesn't stop relatives from arguing about which parent you look like most. But don't worry – they lose interest by the time you become a parent yourself.

Glenn Murphy wrote his first book, *Why is Snot Green?*, while working at the Science Museum, London. Since then he has written around twenty popular-science titles aimed at kids and teens, including the bestselling *How Loud Can You Burp?* and *Space: The Whole Whizz-Bang Story*.

His books are read by brainy children, parents and teachers worldwide, and have been translated into Dutch, German, Spanish, Turkish, Finnish, Chinese, Japanese, Korean and Indonesian, which is kind of awesome. In 2007 he moved to the United States and began writing full-time, which explains why he now says things like 'kind of awesome'.

These days he lives in sunny, leafy North Carolina with his wife Heather, and his son Sean, who asks many marvellous questions.

Al Murphy has drawn pictures for lots of people, including the *Guardian*, the *New York* magazine and the *BBC*, but his favourite thing to do is draw for fun while listening to music and eating chocolate. He likes tomato soup with melted cheese and takes his tea with milk and one sugar.

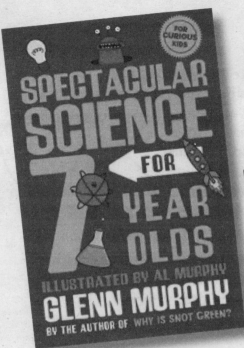

FOR CURIOUS KIDS

SPECTACULAR SCIENCE FOR 7 YEAR OLDS

ILLUSTRATED BY AL MURPHY

GLENN MURPHY

BY THE AUTHOR OF WHY IS SNOT GREEN?

Do spiders have noses?

Why is the Earth shaped like a ball?

How do clouds make lightning?

Why don't magnets stick to everything?

Glenn Murphy, author of
Why Is Snot Green? and *How Loud Can You Burp?*,
is back to answer all the big, small and out-of-this-world
questions in this brilliantly fun and fact-filled book.
Packed with all of the science, medicine and engineering
a 7 year old needs to know.